TABLE OF CONTENTS

How to Start an

AIRBNB
GLAMPING BUSINESS

- THE COMPLETE GUIDE -

to Starting Your Own Short-term Rental Glamping Business Using Tents, Yurts, Airstreams and More!

By **BE THE BOSS ACADEMY**

Disclaimer

This book provides a comprehensive overview of the process involved with starting a glamping business. The information provided is based on personal experience from the author and does not guarantee any specific results for the reader. The reader is advised to use the information and knowledge they obtain in this book at their own risk. The author does not take any responsibility for losses occurring through the information that the reader can obtain in this book. The book does not provide a substitute for professional advice from a career expert or professional business consultant. While the opportunity to start a glamping business is real and can produce a large income, results may vary between readers.

Introduction

Tossing and turning at night, struggling to fall asleep. That was me a few years ago. The worries of finances can really take a toll on your mental and physical health. A nine-to-five job gave me just enough income to ensure I could make ends meet until the time came for my next paycheck.

This is actually something that affects millions of people over the entire world. About 56% of men and 68% of women find that they sometimes struggle to sleep due to stress related to their finances. In the United States, 60% of the population has sleepless nights due to debt, healthcare costs, finances for education, and the inability to save up for retirement.

A majority of these people work regular nine-to-five jobs or sometimes even more extended hours. They live paycheck to paycheck and constantly worry about their future. It is a place where I found myself at one point too, which is why I started to look for methods that could help me earn extra money.

When it comes to starting a business, you need funds - and since we are already worrying about our finances, things can look disappointing at this point. The truth is, you can get started with minimal funds as long as you have the will and choose something that you will enjoy.

For me, the foundation of a glamping business was the ideal opportunity to earn some extra cash and have fun in the process. Glamping is a term that we see more and more of. It refers to a type of camping experience that is "glamorized." When you think of camping, you will generally picture a forest environment or perhaps a lake, along with a tent. These are the essentials of traditional camping but do not suit everyone. Glamping fixes the things that make camping unpleasant for some people and still gives you that classic atmosphere and experience.

THE RISE OF GLAMPING

Glamping is not a new term. It first gained popularity in 2007, when people started to show significant interest in the activity within regions like Europe and the United Kingdom. The term has gained so much interest that there is an official Glamping.com domain, which provides extensive information about glamping sites and experiences that people can enjoy.

We've also seen a consistent increase in interest in glamping experiences, and by 2016, Oxford English Dictionary added the term "glamping" as an official word. These experiences are not only popular in Europe and the UK but are also rising in popularity throughout the United States and other parts of the world. Recent reports also suggest that the worldwide glamping market will likely reach a value of $1 billion by 2024.

The market currently experiences a year-on-year growth of around 12%.

GLAMPING AS A BUSINESS OPPORTUNITY

Glamping is not just something that people enjoy; it also presents an excellent business opportunity. This type of business opportunity gives you the ability to earn extra money while you attend your day job. There are even cases where people are able to break away from the traditional nine-to-five job and earn a comfortable living with the glamping business that they decided to start.

If you are looking for a fun and exciting way to earn money, then setting up your own glamping business is a great way to get going. You don't even need access to an entire park if you want to give your guests a glamorous camping experience. In fact, many of these businesses start out in a backyard and then steadily grow into something bigger.

The major problem that you may face, however, is uncertainty. You can already see just how much opportunity lies in this industry, but you feel unsure about where or how to start if you want to have your own glamping business. The idea of failure is daunting, so you might delay the process due to your uncertainties.

I decided to write this book for this particular reason. I felt unsure and confused when I decided to delve into the world of glamping too. One thing that did help me was the fact that I had already experienced glamping in the past - in fact, this is where I initially learned about my passion for these experiences. Since you are considering this type of business model, you've likely either heard, seen, or experienced glamping for yourself in the past. Now, you want to give other people that same experience.

In this book, we're going to take a look at what it takes to start a glamping business. I'll share with you the troubles I had to face and the challenges that blocked my way, as well as how I was able to overcome them. Today, I have a successful glamping business that allowed me to get away from my traditional job and do something that really inspires me - and this can be you too.

By the end of this book, you'll have the knowledge to set up a glamping business that works. You can avoid the mistakes I made because I'll share them with you. You get a step-by-step process that goes over everything in detail to ensure you don't have any thoughts of uncertainty or confusion but rather feel confident about your ability to start this type of business.

Now, imagine a life where you have more time to spend with your friends, the kids, and your family. A life where you are not trapped by a nine-to-five job that only pays enough so that you can barely scrape through the month. A life where you get the chance to give other people a glamping experience, making them happy and satisfying their desire for adventure- and you get paid to do all of this. These are the goals that I wish to help you achieve through the information, tips, and knowledge I offer in my book.

•

WHY GLAMPING?

Before we get into this chapter, I want to share a quick success story with you. I'm going to take you all the way to Puerto Rico here, where Manolo Ramos decided to set up the area's very first glamping site. Manolo decided on a glamping business structure for both personal and professional reasons, with the decision coming shortly after he became a father. At the time, he was working as a freelancer, which meant he didn't have a consistent income.

One of the most inspiring factors related to Manolo's story is how he began. Manolo didn't have a huge budget to perform mass production of a glamping site. Instead, he had to use his budget to set up just a series of five tents to start with - but this was enough to get his glamping site going.

Today, he owns an award-winning glamping site that many people travel to for the experience. Visitors get to experience the beauty of the Pitahaya Region, all while camping in a glamored-up tent with all the facilities they need to get through the trip.

The lesson here is that you do not have to spend millions of dollars and set up a large glamping site that spans an entire forest if you want to get started. Begin small and take things to step by step - this is the secret to success for many people. Remember that every glamping site you view as an inspiration has to start somewhere. Thus, even if you have to start with your backyard as the campsite, put in the effort, and you can experience growth in your business.

Of course, this is just one of the many examples that show how people start out with minimal assets but, with perseverance, are able to strive toward big goals.

In this chapter, I am going to introduce you to the idea of glamor camping, or glamping, as most people know it today. I am also going to walk you through the profitability that this type of business opportunity presents, and we will take a closer look at the different types of glamping accommodation options that you can use. Providing you with an unbiased view of this industry is important, which is why you will also note I'm going to dive into both the pros and cons of a glamping business in this chapter. This way, you'll have the ability to weigh the benefits and drawbacks of the business model in terms of how it will affect you - and make an informed choice that you won't end up regretting later on.

Glamor Camping

Glamping - a term that combines "glamor" and "camping" - is something that first took note in 2005. In fact, the term was used for the first time in the United Kingdom this year and then started to become more widespread throughout the world from there. While the term is something that we only were introduced to in the 20th century, the idea behind these experiences really dates back to much older times.

First notes of glamor camping date back to around the 16th century. The idea in these times primarily focused on providing tents as living environments but also offering access to luxuries and various essential facilities in these tents. They were described as luxurious tents, and were commonly found between the times of Henry VIII and Francis I. People also called these living environments Field of the Cloth of Gold at the time.

Today, glamping can be described as a modernized version of these accommodation styles.

Glamping is considered an ideal choice for couples as well as people traveling with friends. It is often the solution where one person enjoys backpacking, hiking, and traditional camping, but the other individual would rather stay at a hotel. With glamping, people are provided with the best of both worlds.

Depending on the setup of the glamping environment, some of these tents and structures may even provide access to electricity, lights, and even facilities to cook food. The main idea is to add a luxury touch to a camping trip. The tents themselves often also include special structures that offer better protection against outdoor elements like rain or strong winds.

Are Glamping Businesses Profitable?

The main reason why I decided to write this book is to help you better understand the process of profiting from the glamping industry. You were likely already interested in setting up a glamping business before you decided to pick up this book - but you had some questions that you needed answers to before you decided to move forward.

One of the most common questions that you might have is whether or not this type of business structure is really profitable. In order to determine the profitability of a business, it is important to take several things into consideration. You also need to understand that some people succeed and some people fail - it really comes down to how you get started and whether you do enough planning to ensure you are able to overcome any challenges you face down the road.

Something that you need to consider here is the fact that the glamping industry is consistently rising and is expected to continue growing in the near future. This means the industry is going to continuously present opportunities that you can take advantage of. Thus, the short answer here is yes - the glamping business is profitable. How profitable it is, however, depends on a couple of factors - each of which you need to carefully assess before you decide to make any type of commitment.

. . .

In this section, I am going to discuss some of the most important considerations that help you decide the overall profitability that comes with a glamping business.

START-UP COSTS

The very first thing that you should consider is the costs involved with starting your own glamping business. Now, there is no fixed amount that will cover any type of glamping startup. As I discussed earlier in this chapter, some people start with just a couple of tents. Due to the popularity of glamping, people generally turn to these sites more for the experience. Some people may even start out at home, which can be a good option if you are limited in terms of a startup budget. Later on, you can then decide to expand. This is a feasible option if you have a large backyard that you can use to set up this type of luxury camping site.

Regardless of where or how you will go about setting up a glamping site, there are some important costs that you will need to take care of as you start this type of business.

- **Accommodation Setup:** The initial setup of the accommodation that you are going to provide to your guests will form a major part of the start-up costs. This is a good starting point when you want to determine profitability. The income you receive from your guests needs to make up for the cost of the tents or other structures that you will buy. Bell tents are the cheapest way to go, as the prices for setting up these structures usually start at around $2,000.

- **Property Rental:** If you are going to rent a piece of land to set up your camping site, then you also have to take the rental fees for the area into consideration. This will depend on the location and the size of the land.
- **Utility Setup:** When you want to provide a luxurious camping experience, you have to provide some basic utilities to your guests. This means you will incur expenses for the setup of utilities like a water supply, plumbing, and electricity.
- **Furnishing:** In most cases, glamping sites offer access to furnished accommodation. Depending on the type of experience you wish to provide your guests with, you may need to buy beds, mattresses, stretchers, bedding items, and towels. Some of these facilities also offer outdoor furniture, which allows the guests to sit down, relax, and enjoy themselves on comfortable chairs outside.

There are sometimes also licensing fees and permits that you need to pay for. Make sure you do not overlook these. Additionally, taking out insurance for your glamping business is also an important factor that you have to attend to. This can help to provide coverage in the case of damage to your property and certain other events.

Growth Rate

The growth rate of an industry or market can provide you with a good overview of how profitable a business can be.

Fortunately, the glamping industry has experienced consistent growth for the past few years. This growth continues to remain present, with an annual increase of over 10%. The industry is also expected to become a billion-dollar market in the next two years.

The glamping markets are biggest in Europe and North America at the moment, but there is momentum in other areas of the world too. Thus, regardless of where you live, the growth rate will continue. Take the example of Manolo that I shared with you before. He started the very first glamping site in Puerto Rico. This means there wasn't already a market there, yet his idea to start a glamping site turned out to be a huge success - and his business now continues to grow.

MARKETING COSTS

When you want to set up a glamping business, there is no use in going through the entire process if nobody knows about it. This is where marketing comes in - and the process of getting your name out there can be costly in some cases. The fees for marketing can be especially high in areas where you face a lot of competition.

Most people who decide to set up a glamping business will decide to have a website designed for their company. This means you need to consider the fees for a domain, the hosting of the website, and the development process. You may also need to hire a graphic designer for a logo. These all form part of the marketing process, along with campaigns that can help you get some initial guests to visit your glamping site.

Operational Costs

Operational costs include those fees that you will need to constantly cover as the business continues to run. This includes payments to staff members, continuous licensing renewal fees, paying for electricity and water, and more. You may also want to get a laundry service to ensure sheets are kept clean. Insurance fees are also part of operational costs, as this is usually a cost that occurs monthly.

Other Costs And Considerations

As the industry grows, trends change, and so do the expectations and requirements of guests that visit glamping sites. This is why you also need to keep in mind other expenses that may come up while you run your glamping business.

Even though there are many expenses to think about, with planning and appropriate research, you can turn a significant profit with a glamping business. You do need to ensure you are realistic with the goals you set for your business, as you won't see a huge profit after just the first few guests. It generally takes a bit of time before the income you get from the business covers for the start-up costs, as well as the operational expenses. With patience, however, you can usually cross this line after a few months, especially if you do proper marketing and get a significant number of guests to stay at your glamping site.

Types Of Glamping Accommodation

When the term "glamping" just started to surface, it generally referred to camping but with some added glamor or luxury. In its earlier stages, glamping was only used to describe camping sites that used traditional tents, along with access to certain facilities. Today, however, glamping is a much more versatile term that people use to describe different types of accommodation facilities.

Still, bell tents remain the most common type of accommodation that includes a glamping experience. These tents are less expensive than some of the other options and can provide a safe environment for guests to wind down and enjoy nature. Depending on the design of a bell tent, it can also be used to provide guests access to comfortable furniture, bathrooms, kitchens, and several other facilities.

There are, of course, other types of glamping accommodation options that are available in the modern day. Let's take a closer look at a few of the accommodation types that people often look for, apart from the standard bell tent:

- **Tiny Homes:** Tiny homes have been a trending topic for quite some time now. In fact, I've found myself quite interested in a few TV shows that specifically focus on tiny homes. They are beautiful, compact, and quite easy to set up. Due to the expanding scope of glamping, many people use tiny homes in order to provide people with these experiences. A tiny home can provide guests access to a diverse range of facilities, all packed into a compact apartment-like structure. These homes can also be set up anywhere - including forest regions where people can feel like they are camping, but without the need to use a classic tent. Tiny homes generally range from around $4,000 to $6,000 to set up, but due to the creative options you have with these facilities, you can usually ask more per night for guests who want to stay at your glamping site.

- **Treehouses:** Another type of accommodation that has become quite popular among people who want to go glamping is treehouses. These are basically small house-like structures that are built onto a tree. You do need to get the right location with strong tree stumps if this is the way that you would like to go. The tree should be able to hold the structure of the home, along with some support slabs that go down the sides. A treehouse will often be one of the more expensive types of accommodations to set up, but it can provide a luxurious experience to the guests.

Other than these, some glamping sites also make use of A-frame tent kits and shed to provide accommodation to guests. Some of these sites also use gypsy caravans, huts, tipis, teepees, and yurts to provide accommodation. One very effective strategy is to combine different types of accommodation on a single site. This can give guests more versatility when they want to choose the type of experience that they would like to have at the facility. This would also allow you to optimize the packages that you present to your guests based on the budget that they have available.

. . .

There are several unique options that you can also explore, as these can add a creative touch to your glamping grounds. A few examples of unique options that can be seen at some of the glamping areas around the world include:

- Domes and bubbles
- Caves
- Igloos
- Floating homes

While these do require a more significant initial investment, they might end up providing a greater attraction for people who want to visit different glamping spots. In turn, this could have a positive outcome on the overall results of your business and attract people from a wider range to visit your site.

Advantages (and Drawbacks) of a Glamping Business

When you want to start a new business, it is critical to ensure you are both unbiased and realistic about the process. This accounts for a glamping business too. You need to understand what it takes, what the benefits are, and the potential risks and drawbacks that you may face.

This is why I decided to have a specific section dedicated to discussing both the pros and cons of a glamping business. These factors are geared toward starting a glamping business but will still remain present as your business grows over time. When you weigh these to each other, you get a clearer picture of what you should expect from this type of business opportunity. You'll be able to understand whether a glamping business is really for you and if you are capable of taking risks.

We will start with the benefits that come with a glamping business:

- **Rewarding Work:** It is true that you want to start a glamping business for professional and financial reasons, but most people who do also enjoy glamping themselves. This means you will have fun doing your job but still be rewarded for your actions at the same time.
- **Business Connections:** Glamping sites are experiences that many people seek out. You can use this to your advantage. Sometimes, you might even meet business prospects, investors, or other like-minded individuals when you have a quick chat with guests who arrive at your site.
- **Physical Activity:** When you have a glamping business, you will generally need to move around a lot. From running a few small errands to checking up on your guests, these are all things that you will do throughout the day. This means a glamping business is a great opportunity to keep yourself physically active and work on your fitness.
- **Perks:** There are certain perks that you can get access to when you decide to start your own glamping business. When you buy certain products in bulk, you can enjoy large discounts. If you register your business, then there are also certain companies who may provide you with

special discounts and perks if you decide to make them your supplier for specific products.

- **Work For Yourself:** With a glamping business, there is no need to constantly report to your superiors, such as a supervisor or manager. You are your own boss and only need to report to yourself. This can reduce the stress you have when you go about your daily routine, as you do not have someone constantly watching over your shoulder.
- **Referrals:** Marketing plays a crucial role in the success of a glamping business. When you are able to impress your guests with a great experience, then you can start to rely on free word-of-mouth marketing. Guests will refer other people to your site to ensure their friends can also enjoy what your glamping business has to offer.
- **Human Interactions:** Most people who own a glamping business will prefer to greet guests as they arrive at the site. This gives you an opportunity to have face-to-face conversations, which makes the business great for those who like to interact with customers and other people.
- **Simple Business:** The business model for a glamping site is relatively simple, especially when you compare it to some of the other businesses that you can start. This means you do not need exceptional expertise in business management and related aspects to get started with your glamping company.
- **Variety:** Many owners of a glamping business will agree that there never really is a dull moment. You meet all kinds of people from different backgrounds and cultures. These are moments that many people enjoy, as they get to experience

diversity instead of seeing the same people in an office environment every day.

- **Extra Income Streams:** With a glamping business, there are also several opportunities for extra revenue that often present themselves. You can become part of a local community with support when you need it. Once your business lifts off, make branded items that are useful for people who want to create their own glamping sites and sell this at local markets. This allows you to promote your business and earn extra money at the same time.

While there are numerous benefits, let's also consider the drawbacks that you have to keep in mind before you start taking action:

- Finding suppliers for a glamping business can sometimes be tough, especially if you are just starting out. You may need to pay full prices at the beginning of your business and build up relationships with suppliers first. This can add to the overall expenses you have during that early phase.
- As the market continues to grow, so does your competition. People are quickly adapting to the idea of glamping, and there are new businesses being set up consistently.
- It's hard to work with employees sometimes and to keep them motivated. This is another obstacle that you may face as your business expands.

- When you decide to start a glamping business, then you may find you need to pay a lot of taxes. This is because most tax authorities will recognize you as a self-employed individual in these situations.
- The profit margin for the average glamping business is also not that high, weighing in at around 43%. This means it might be hard to buy new items and expand early on.
- The initial expenses can be a bit high for some people, especially if you do not already own a space where you can set up these glamping facilities.

KEY CONSIDERATIONS BEFORE STARTING

Once you've set your mind on starting a glamping business, there are a couple of considerations that you have to consider. When you take a few key considerations into account before you start out, you will generally have a better chance at success. This can also help you get a more realistic overview of what you should expect, how long it will take to be successful, and more.

Here are some of the most important considerations that you should not overlook:

- Location really is everything when it comes to starting a glamping business. Choose an area that provides a beautiful view of nature and the perfect "campy" feeling. You should ideally pick an area that also gets a lot of traffic, as this can help to ease the process of promoting your business.

- Keep in mind the motivation you have behind the idea of starting this business. For some, it's the money that comes with the opportunity. Others may rather focus on their love for nature and glamping in general. There are also people who have both of these motivations in mind.
- Consider the costs that you will incur to start the business initially and determine how this will affect you financially. At this point, it is important to consider whether you are able to start out right away or, rather, need to save up for a few months before you make your move.
- Make sure you keep in mind that glamping businesses are about more than just making money. They also help you provide an experience for your guests and give you something fun to do as a job.

We looked at what glamping is and how profitable a glamping business can be in this chapter. In the next chapter, I will tell you all about how you can do market research to help you identify the right location and type of accommodation and how to reach your target market accurately and effectively.

CONDUCT MARKET
RESEARCH

In May 2021, Braeview Glamping was launched for the public to access after a month of private access to assess the site and provide the owner's with feedback. This is just one other example of a glamping business that really took off and became something successful - with the owners now getting more requests for accommodation than they thought they would have.

Morgan and her husband, both of whom now serve as the owners of Braeview Glamping, weren't always interested in glamping particularly. Instead, they really enjoyed a more traditional camping experience. When the two got married, they even spent their honeymoon in a tent. After visiting a camping site where a glamping pod was available for accommodation, the two had a breakthrough idea. After some discussion, Morgan and her husband decided it was time for a change in their lifestyle, but they didn't want to give up camping altogether.

. . .

Instead of going on glamping adventures themselves, the couple rather decided to set up their own business. They did have to go through a series of time-consuming tasks in order to present the feasibility of the land to Morgan's mother, as she was the owner of the land they had set out to use for the glamping business. Following these events, the couple was able to create a glamping site solely focused on adults, which is the unique selling point that they decided on. Today, Braeview Glamping continues to thrive - and a great deal of this success is related to the fact that the owner's conducted efficient market research to ensure they knew what to do and how to overcome every obstacle in their way.

This chapter entirely focuses on the important role that market research plays when it comes to starting a glamping business. We are going to take a look at how the business model you choose will affect your glamping site, where you should set up a glamping spot, how you can identify and specify your target market, and what steps are involved in competitor research.

BUSINESS MODEL

When you want to set up your own glamping site, it is important to understand that this will be an actual business. You need to register your business and obtain adequate licensing from your local state governments. This means you will need to pick the right business model before you proceed with anything else. Choosing the right business model early on can make things much easier later on - and also ensure you understand what you need to do to get your company off the ground.

. . .

There are a couple of different business models that you are able to consider when setting up a glamping business. This may all feel a bit confusing, especially if you have not owned a company before. Certain business models can provide you with personal protection in cases where things do not go as planned, which reduces the risk you place on your own assets. There are also certain business models that can provide a glamping company with benefits and access to certain services or facilities.

CONDUCT MARKET RESEARCH

Market research starts to play a part in the process even at this point. With thorough market research, you can start to find out more about how each type of business model can benefit you. It also allows you to compare the benefits and drawbacks of various business models for a glamping site. In the end, market research can help you make a more informed choice during this particular phase of the process.

The first step here is to take a closer look at who your competitors are. When you decide to start a glamping business, having the scope on your competitors is crucial. This allows you to note only see who you are up against, but also learn from how they run their own businesses.

At this point, you should consider the type of business models other glamping sites in the area use. If you find that the options are limited with glamping sites in your area, then expand your search to a larger radius. There are a couple of common business models that people decide to opt for when it comes to starting a glamping business, but you should focus on the ones that are most appropriate for your start-up company.

Franchise

One of the easiest ways to get into the glamping industry is to opt for a franchise-type business model. This process generally involves setting up a glamping zone under an existing brand's name. There are a couple of franchises that allow you to apply to open your own branch, but it is important to fully understand what you should expect from this type of business model.

The main benefits that you can expect from a franchise include the following:

- You can take advantage of an existing brand name, which could definitely give you an edge with a glamping business.
- You get support from the franchise owner. In some cases, you may also receive marketing materials and even a complete booking system to make the management of your business easier.
- The franchise owner might also help you find a suitable location and provide you with some initial market research that you can use to ease this initial phase of setting up the business.

While it may seem like an attractive opportunity, it is important to note that you will require quite a substantial initial capital if you choose to use a franchise business model. You may be required to pay an initial fee and have a certain amount of capital in your bank before the franchise owner approves your application. Additionally, there are higher operating costs involved with this business model. There are usually continuous franchising and commission fees that you have to pay on a regular basis, which makes it harder to keep this type of glamping business model profitable.

Corporation

When it comes to setting up everything from scratch without utilizing an existing brand in the glamping industry, then a corporation is a popular choice. This particular type of glamping business generally relies on funds from investors. These investors will usually form the board of directors that are involved in the management and decision-making within the business. It is a good choice for people who decide to ask investors to assist with providing initial funds for their glamping business.

If you intend to get investors on board, then you have to ensure you carefully approach the entire process. You need a solid business plan with accurate financial data and forecasts before you will be able to find investors willing to work with you.

Sole Proprietorship

When you are going to be the only person who owns the business, then a sole proprietorship is usually the best choice to go with. You do need to understand, however, that this particular business model means you and the business are not two separate legal entities. Thus, the risks you take for the business will also reflect on your personal life, which means there are greater risks and challenges that you may face.

The great thing about a sole proprietorship, however, is the fact that you are able to keep the profits for yourself and do not have to pay commission fees or share it with a board of directors or investors.

LLC

Another option that you can also consider is to register your glamping business as a limited liability company, or LLC for short. This type of business provides you with personal liability protection, similar to that of a corporation. It also gives you the taxation benefits that come with the registration of a sole proprietorship. This is actually a very popular and common business structure to find - not only for glamping sites but also for other types of companies.

WHAT ARE THE GLAMPING BUSINESS TYPES AND OPTIONS?

While it is important to ensure you choose the right glamping business model, you also have to consider the type of company that you would like to establish. There is a significant variation of opportunities that you can find in the glamping industry. You do need to analyze all of these opportunities and pick a business type that is suitable for your project.

. . .

Once you have chosen a specific business model to follow, the next step is to consider the type of glamping site structure that you wish to use. This particular decision will also play a large role later on as you go through each step of the process before you open up your glamping site to the public.

- **Resort Developments:** This can be a good choice if you have a very large budget available. A resort development usually consists of many units that customers can rent, and often offers access to additional facilities like restaurants, a pool, spas, and other options.
- **Private SME:** Most of the glamping businesses that people start as an individual will be a type of private small-to-medium business, also known as a private SME. This allows you to use land that you already own or to buy existing land with the goal of setting up a glamping site. These businesses are often family-owned.
- **Supplementary Accommodation:** If you already own a type of establishment, then you could consider adding glamping sites as supplementary accommodation. For example, a hotel owner might decide to diversify the accommodation options that they offer with the addition of a glamping area.
- **Attractions:** Theme parks and other attractions can also consider the use of glamping sites to get people to stay longer.
- **Pop-Up Sites:** You could also consider offering temporary glamping solutions for events that will only last for a short period of time. For example,

when there is a music festival, you can offer the setup of pop-up glamping solutions and have everything ready by the time the guests arrive.

- **Hire Options:** Apart from the options that we discussed, another opportunity relies on the use of rented land in order to develop a glamping site. In this case, you will not outright buy a piece of land but rather rent it from its existing owner. You may find that you have more restrictions in terms of how you can modify the land for your business, but it is a viable option if you do not have the funds to buy a piece of land right away.

LOCATION

When it comes to a glamping business, location really is everything. Choose the wrong location to set up your glamping site, and you'll have quite a hard time getting people to notice your business and book stays at your facility. This is why location should form part of your market research early on.

There is no perfect location for every type of glamping site. You have to consider a couple of things in order to determine where you should position your glamping site. Availability of land can also often cause problems, but there are methods to work around these challenges and still choose a good location.

In this section, we are going to take a closer look at a couple of things that you should prioritize when you decide to look for the right location to set up your glamping site.

Check For The Perfect Location

You should first consider the specific properties that would make a piece of land perfect for a glamping site. This can help to provide your customers with peace of mind and take their safety into consideration at the same time.

Below, we take a look at a couple of properties and characteristics that you should define during this process:

- It is important to consider how far the location is from the closest city. This gives people a good idea about how long they will need to drive before they are able to reach a specific city. People often do not want to drive too far when they need to access grocery stores or supermarkets while they are on a glamping trip.
- Safety should always be a priority, which is why you also need to consider how far away these sites are from medical facilities. Emergency situations can happen unexpectedly while people are taking advantage of the facilities you have at your glamping site.
- In addition to ensuring the site is close enough to medical facilities, you should also ensure the environment will provide easy access for emergency services. This way, when you do need to call an ambulance, they will not struggle to get onto the glamping site.
- The view that the camps that you set up on the site offer is also very important. Remember that

people generally turn to glamping sites for the experience. When they sit down inside their camp, these people want a great view of mother nature.

- Apart from these factors, you also need to consider the risks of calamities in the area. Choose lands that are not prone to earthquakes, fires, landslides, tsunamis, and other natural disasters. This can further help to contribute toward the safety of your customers.

YOUR DESIRED GLAMPING LOCATION

While there are some things that you need to consider about the characteristics of various land pieces, you should also keep in mind the region where you are going to set up the site. Every area comes with its own rules and regulations that you have to follow when you decide to start a glamping business.

During the assessment period, especially when you choose where you want to position the site, be sure to keep the following in mind:

- **Weather:** When people visit your glamping site for a great experience, they don't want to have rainy days throughout their entire trip. This is why you have to consider the weather conditions in each area you look at. Search for areas where there is not as much rain and snowy days throughout the year.
- **Regulations:** Each state has its own set of regulations regarding the setup of glamping

businesses and sites. You will have to fully comply with these regulations if you wish to set up a glamping site. Make sure you carefully consider the regulations of every area and see how they could restrict your ability to run a glamping business. Compare these regulations with the expectations and plans that you have for your glamping site.

- **Costs:** The land ownership and rental prices also differ from one region to the next. This is another thing that you will need to keep in mind when you assess different locations that you can use.

Glamping Without Owning Land

Let's face it - not everyone owns a piece of land that they can easily give up to set up a glamping business. It's also a huge expense if you want to buy a piece of land for this purpose. When your budget for starting a glamping business is limited, then there is generally no way to buy a piece of land for your site.

Luckily, there are alternatives that you can explore. You do not have to own land necessarily when you want to set up a glamping business. There are certain options, such as co-hosting, that you can look at. Perhaps someone owns a piece of land and is interested in setting up a glamping site, but does not have the knowledge or experience to do so. This is where you come in, as you can offer some capital and your expertise in order to help them develop a glamping site. Another alternative is to rent a piece of land. There have also been cases where people started out with their backyard as a glamping site and then gradually expanded from there.

Purchasing An Existing Campsite

If you have some initial funds, but do not want to explore options like a franchise, then you can consider the purchase of an existing campsite. There are many campsites all over the world and many of them only offer their customers basic facilities. This, however, means less work for you in order to convert the campsite into a glamping business. You'll generally be able to utilize the existing facilities that the current owner of the campsite has implemented and you can then simply expand on what is already there.

Target Market

One of the most important aspects of market research is to fully understand your target audience. In order to understand the audience that you will target with your glamping site, however, you first need to identify them. There are a couple of factors that you can keep in mind in order to help you find your target audience and gain a better understanding of who they are, their habits, and other important factors.

Key Driving Factors For Glamping

The first thing is to identify the key driving factors for people who are interested in glamping. Festivals and concerts are a driving factor for many people. When people decide to attend a festival that is not close to their home, they might look for a glamping site in order to have a camp-like experience nearby the location of the concert or festival. Of course, other driving factors also exist, such as a thirst for adventure among those who look for glamping zones.

Who Likes Glamping?

Identifying your target audience also means defining where they come from and their age. The glamping market is largest within Europe, which means people from countries in Europe are the most likely to look for glamping sites. Additionally, North America also holds a large share of the glamping industry.

In terms of age, research shows that people between the age of 18 and 55 make up around 70% of all individuals who go on glamping trips. This means your strategies should have a large focus on people within this age range.

Main Characteristics Of These Generations

Once you are able to identify the people who are most likely to visit your glamping sites, it is important to optimize your business for them. Here are a few statistics that are generally shared among the generations and age group most interested in glamping activities:

- These people are internet savvy and love technology in many cases. This means they want access to facilities like Wi-Fi internet and other technology-related features.
- Traveling is often a priority for people who go on glamping trips.

In addition to optimizing your site, you can also use this data in order to ensure you can effectively reach your target audience on the devices that they use most.

COMPETITIVE ANALYSIS

The final part of your market research is where competitive analysis comes in. While you have already gone through a couple of processes to identify the right location for your glamping site and to learn more about your target audience, you should also get a better view of your competitors. By assessing every competitor, it is much easier to understand what you should avoid and things that can help to give your company a boost.

STEPS TO PERFORMING A COMPETITIVE ANALYSIS

A competitive analysis should ideally be as detailed as possible. This will give you more information to work with and also allows you to find an opportunity to create a competitive advantage or a unique selling point that attracts customers to your glamping site. We will take a closer look at a few important steps that will help you effectively analyze your competitors.

IDENTIFY COMPETITORS

Start by defining and identifying who your competitors are. This is a very important step in the process, as you cannot perform an analysis if you do not know who you are up against with your glamping business.

. . .

There are a few strategies that you can use for this particular process, but it is best to take your search online. Look for "glamping sites" in your area on Google and other search areas, then start to make a list of them. It is a good idea to collect the names and details of multiple glamping businesses in your area. This will give you more data to work with when you conduct a comprehensive competitor analysis.

Analyze Competitors' Online Presence

Once you have a few competitors in a list, start by taking a closer look at their online presence. Technology is booming and that is why these companies will often focus on their digital marketing strategies to draw in customers. Look at the social media platforms that each of these companies uses, as well as the type of content that they post. You should also visit the website of every competitor, as you can find useful information about their campsites, the type of glamping accommodation they use, and the facilities they offer their clients. Use this information to get some details about pricing at your competitors' facilities too.

Check Online Reviews

While you assess the online presence of your competitors, it is important to look for reviews. These reviews are not only useful for new customers who are looking for a glamping site, but can also be valuable when you conduct a competitor analysis during your market research phase.

Talk To Competitors' Customers

When you find poor reviews on the competitor's online properties, then consider contacting the clients. You can ask them about their experience, what they didn't like, and what they would want to improve. With this type of information, you can easily avoid similar reviews in the future, as you would offer a more personalized approach to glamping.

IDENTIFY THEIR STRENGTHS AND WEAKNESSES

You have to attempt to identify the strengths and weaknesses of every competitor that you analyze through this process. The main idea here is to understand what elements you should focus on and identify specific areas where you could improve your own glamping business. You should address the weaknesses that you identify among your competitors when you develop a business plan for your glamping company.

USE RESEARCH TOOLS

It is important to use the right tools when you decide to perform a competitor analysis. You can use tools like SEMRush and Ahrefs when you want to get an idea about the online marketing strategies these businesses use, as well as the keywords they rank for. Take advantage of cloud-based document processing software, such as Google Docs, to develop a business plan. This way, you won't experience data loss in the event where your computer dies or you run into other similar problems. Google Sheets is also great for setting up spreadsheets, which you can use for financials and several other types of competitor data.

Now that you understand how to do proper market research, it is time to take the first steps to get your business going. In the next chapter, I will give you some guidance as to how you can use the data you collect during this section to create a business plan. You will discover the most important elements of a business plan and learn more about the registration process for your glamping site.

Business Plan And Registration

After Lord Edmund Limerick expressed his interest in the glamping industry during a show in 2020, he started working with a consultant in order to get things going. During his journey, Lord Edmund Limerick decides to set up a glamping business on an existing site. There were already pool facilities, as well as a brewery on the property. The same property had a building where people held certain events, such as weddings.

Lord Limerick decided to go with domes as the accommodation type on the property. These domes provide a great outlook on the fields while also offering the guests easy access to the facilities that were already on the property.

Prior to taking any actions, however, Lord Limerick, along with the consultants hc hired, worked on comprehensive market research and focused on producing a business plan.

While setting up a business plan took some time, it is now helping to ensure every step is implemented at the right time and by following the right process.

This is a great example of the role that a business plan plays in the process of starting a new company - and it accounts for any type of glamping business that you might decide to start. This entire chapter revolves around the importance of a business plan for your glamping site. You will discover how you can write a business plan and the different segments that you should add. I will also guide you through some of the initial preparation steps that you have to take before you start to implement any actions to get your glamping business started.

This will help to give you an upper hand when it comes to setting up your glamping site and preparing to open it to the public.

Preparing A Business Plan

The first step here is to develop a business plan. This plays an important role for a number of reasons. When you have a business plan, it is easier to talk to investors in order to get funding if you do not have the required capital to start this type of company. If you decide to register as a sole proprietor and need some extra funds, a good credit score, along with a proper business plan, can also help you secure the required money from a bank or other lending institute.

Do not take your business plan lightly. If needed and you do not have the expertise required, then get a professional to help you with this particular process. This will ensure you can set up a professional business plan that is worth looking at for banks, financial institutes, and investors. Even in scenarios where you have the funding required to set up the glamping site without the need for extra finances, you should still get a business plan together. This will ensure you do not run into trouble when you register your business, apply for a tax number, or take out insurance and are required to submit certain documents.

During the initial step, you'll need to conduct some research and set up the overall layout of your business plan. Collect and record any data you find during research to ensure you can refer to this at a later point.

Writing Your Glamping Business Plan

Your glamping business is a company as a whole, even in cases where you decide to be the sole owner and register as a sole proprietor. When it comes to writing a glamping business plan, it is important to understand what each section means, the importance of every piece, and what goes into each of these plans.

We will start with three of the most essential, as they are a great starting point for your glamping business plan. These three can also help to provide you with data that you can later on use as you fill out more sections in the business plan that you develop.

EXECUTIVE SUMMARY

The very first thing that you need to add to your business plan, apart from ensuring you use a proper layout, is the executive summary. If you have viewed a business plan in the past, you already know just how long these documents can take. When you submit a business plan for investors, a financial institute, an insurance company, or another authority, they do not always want to read through the entire document right away. This is why professionals and investors will generally view the executive summary of the plan before they dive into the documents themselves.

Make sure the executive summary is close to the front of the business plan. This will ensure those viewing the plan can easily access it without having to search for this particular part of the document.

There are a couple of things that you have to cover in your executive summary. This will ensure anyone who needs to review the business plan can gather the data they require to make certain decisions easily.

- **Introduction:** The introduction of the glamping business plan should provide enough information so that the reader can instantly see what your company is all about. Start with a brief summary of what makes your glamping business idea special. In the introduction, you should also provide an overview of any credentials that makes you worthy of starting a glamping business. This may include experience in the hospitality industry in general or managing rental businesses in the past.

- **Motivations:** The executive summary also needs to provide information about why you decided to start a glamping business. Be concise and to the point. Do not provide an entire story about your experiences at sites and how you came to realize you wanted to start this type of business. Rather state your interests and the objectives that you have for this company.

- **Target Market Summary:** Research is important for any business to thrive, so make sure you already provide evidence of your capabilities to conduct market research early on. While you compile the executive summary, provide a brief overview of the target audience that you will focus on with your business. The summary should also offer details about problems that your target market may have, such as the need for accommodation when they travel to attend concerts or other events. Then, describe how your glamping business will solve these issues.

- **Market Research Summary:** In the final part of the executive summary, provide a quick overview of the results you obtained when you performed market research - which I outlined in the previous chapter of this book. This will further provide important selling points for the reader to consider when they assess your business plan.

MARKET AND REVENUE POTENTIAL RESEARCH

When you want to involve investors or get funds in another manner for your glamping site, then you essentially have to provide evidence of the profitability that the company offers. This is why market research is so important. After your executive research, it is important to provide an overview of the market research you conducted and give the reader and investors an idea about the potential revenue you may gain with the site.

The previous chapter discussed the importance of market research and provided an overview of the most important elements to consider. Use the information you gather through the details that I discussed to help you set up this section of your business plan.

A few of the most important things to note here include the following:

- The value and potential of glamping in the area where you will set up the glamping site.
- Trends that you discovered in both rental and glamping industries within the local environment.
- The estimated revenue of other glamping sites that are also situated in a close perimeter to your ideal location.
- The overall saturation of glamping in the area.
- Overview of weather conditions in the local area.

Undertake Competitive Analysis

In Chapter 2 of this book, I also gave you the knowledge you require to do effective competitor analysis. Now is the time to put this data to paper. Use the information that you gather while you perform competitive analysis in order to set up a section that offers a summarized overview of your findings.

This particular section should touch on the following topics:

- The number of competitors in the local region.
- Summarize the strengths and weaknesses of your competitors.
- Provide an overview of the overall success that your competitors show.
- Summarize the marketing strategies that competitors in the local area use.
- Offer details about the target audience each of these competitors focuses on.

After you provide details about these factors related to your competitors, it is also important to add data related to how you will get your own glamping business to stand out from the crowd. This is a difficult position for many people, especially in cases where the market feels a bit saturated in the local area.

Important Business Plan Sections

Now that you have completed the initial part of the business plan, the next step is to divide the document into different sections. Each of these sections technically forms its own plan inside the business plan. This is why you should ensure you are extensive with each section. The more concise and accurate data you can present, the easier it usually is to get investors on board or to use other methods that can help you secure the funding you will later require to get your business going.

The most important sections here include customer analysis, a marketing plan, an operations plan, and financial plans. We take a closer look at each of these separately below.

Customer Analysis

The first section includes a comprehensive customer analysis, which plays a very important role in ensuring you know who your target audience is. The customer analysis will provide comprehensive details about the people who are most likely to visit your glamping site.

In this section, you should present details based on the research that you have conducted. Try to pin down information like the following points to make it clear who will use your business:

- Any specific unique selling points that might affect who your target audience is.

- Whether your target audience is different or similar to that of other glamping sites in the area.
- An overview of the age range that is most likely to use your glamping site for accommodation.
- Details about whether your glamping business will be family friendly or more oriented toward adults who want an escape at a campsite.
- Provide details about whether your business will be pet friendly, as this would also have an impact on defining your target audience.

MARKETING PLAN

Once your business opens up to the public, marketing will play a major role in ensuring its success. In fact, without marketing, people won't be aware of your business - and that means no traffic and visits to your glamping site.

If you want to start a glamping business, you should know how you are going to promote your site before you open its doors. In fact, it is always a good idea to start with the promotion a while before the site opens to the public. This builds up some initial awareness and allows you to run a few promotions to get some initial people to visit your glamping business. While you may not make a full profit on promotional offers, it helps with word-of-mouth marketing and can get you a few initial reviews - and good reviews are always great for this kind of business.

The marketing plan that you add to your business plan should be comprehensive and cover every aspect, including the costs involved with each of your strategies. Provide details about a website that you may develop, a booking system, social media managers, paid ad campaigns, and other aspects. Make sure to also include any local marketing programs that you wish to implement here as well.

Investors will generally take a closer look at the marketing plan you have in mind to determine how easy it will be for customers to find your business. Additionally, you can also use this marketing plan that you compile as a reference point when you start to implement strategies to get your glamping company's name out there.

OPERATIONS PLAN

The operations plan is next and particularly focuses on what happens once you open the doors of your glamping business. While the planning phase is tedious and time-consuming, you need to ensure you understand that things won't calm down once you allow people to stay at your glamping site. For many people, this is when the "real" work starts - and you have to ensure you are thoroughly prepared.

When you compile this particular plan, it is important that you outline all of the operations that you need to focus on when your business is running. This may include:

- Staff and employment factors. This includes the staff members you need in order to run various aspects of your business.

- Details about the maintenance of the facilities that you offer your guests.
- Day-to-day tasks that ensure guests are able to enjoy their stay. This includes room cleaning services, laundry services, and more.
- Maintenance of other on-site facilities, such as a swimming pool or lounge area that guests are allowed to use.
- Regularly costs related to your domain, website hosting, and consistent improvements or additions to your online properties.
- The ongoing costs of your marketing plan should also be summarized here, as it also forms part of the operations that you need to implement continuously to keep your business running.

FINANCIAL PLAN

This is a particularly important part of your glamping business plan and something that you should carefully compile. The financials of your business, including the startup costs, operating expenses, and potential income, are important factors that investors will want to see before they consider providing funds as assistance. Your financial plan can also provide financial institutes with an estimate on the profitability that your business model poses and help them make an informed choice when assessing an application for funds.

In the financial plan, be sure to separate income and expenses. Then, after you focus on these two factors, you should also provide a detailed overview of the potential revenue you can generate with the glamping business.

REGISTER FOR TAXES

Now that you have compiled a business plan, the next step of the process is to register for taxes. This is a very important part of the planning process, as you will be liable for paying taxes when you set up your glamping business. Failure to register and pay your taxes could lead to large fines and legal issues in the future. By now, you should have a good idea about the business structure that you are going to use. You should use this information in order to better understand the process of registering your business for taxes.

APPLY FOR AN EIN

The first step before you can start paying taxes is to apply for an EIN number. The great news is that you do not have to pay any fees if you want to register and obtain an EIN for your business. There are also different methods that you can use here. Visit the IRS's official website to get started. You can also visit a local IRS office or complete the registration through mail. The digital method is, however, a preferred option as it makes the process of submitting returns and paying your taxes much easier.

SMALL BUSINESS TAXES

When you are only starting out with your glamping business, then you are likely classified as a small business. This means you will need to look at different small business taxes that are payable. The structure you chose for your business will come into play here. For example, you may need to pay taxes under regulations for an S Corp, C Corp, LLC, Sole Proprietorship, or a Corporation.

Bank Account, Business Accounting & Permits

When it comes to running a business, even as a sole proprietor, it is important to keep business and personal finances separate. This is why you should ensure you start out early on with a dedicated business account. Setting up your accounting system and obtaining the required permits at this stage is also important. This can help to avoid running into issues later on.

Open A Business Bank Account

The first step is to open up a business bank account. Since you are only starting your business, do not try to apply for a business credit card alongside this account. Your application will likely be rejected, as you first need to work on your business credit. You should also not be too hasty with this step but rather shop around and see what business account offers are available in various institutes. Choosing a business bank account that charges minimal fees is really important at this stage. This can help to keep your early business expenses low. Look at the monthly account fees and transaction fees that each of these bank accounts charges.

Set Up Business Accounting

Accounting plays a crucial part in managing your business, so make sure you set up a system early on. It is definitely a good idea to look at cloud-based accounting solutions. Some of these solutions allow you to get started for free and then, later on, upgrade as the requirements of your business expands. If you are not sure about this step, then you should get an accountant to help with the setup of your business accounting system. Integrations with customer management systems can also be beneficial at this point.

OBTAIN NECESSARY PERMITS AND LICENSES

You need to get the right permits and licenses before you decide to open your doors to the public. The earlier you apply and obtain these licenses, the better. This gives you peace of mind as you implement the other steps that are needed to get your business up. You need to enquire at your local state to determine the specific permits and licenses that are required for a glamping campsite. There are certain associations that can provide you with helpful details in terms of permits, certifications, and licenses.

BUSINESS INSURANCE

Any type of business, including a glamping site, has its risks. This is something that you have to keep in mind during the initial process. Obtaining insurance for your business is critical, as this can help to provide protection in unforeseen events. Start with a plan that offers general liability insurance for your business. You should also consider options like worker's compensation insurance and other products that can help to provide you with an adequate level of protection.

In this chapter, we looked at the important role that a business plan plays. We also looked at some early steps that you should take to provide better security for your business - ultimately contributing to the chances of success you have. The next section is all about securing finances for your glamping business. Without an adequate amount of funds, it is nearly impossible to get things going. We'll assess the different financing options you can explore to secure your business from the start.

Secure Financing

As 2015 came to an end, Ilaeka Villa was able to open the doors of her very own glamping site, along with her father. The two moved from France more than a decade prior to this time and decided to set up a campsite in Tennessee. At the time, Grandview Mountain Cottages consisted of standard cottages and provided a standard accommodation option for travelers.

After discovering an interest in glamping, Ilaeka wanted to implement her own glamping options at Grandview Mountain Cottages. Unfortunately, she did not have either the technical knowledge or the budget to do so. After discussing her options with a consultancy, she was able to secure financing that helped her achieve her dreams of adding glamping facilities to the campsite.

This is just one example of how financing can help not only establish a glamping business but also facilitate growth in the future. Setting up a glamping site is not cheap, which is why many people may not have the initial funds that they need to set up this type of business. Fortunately, there are several types of financing solutions that you can turn to if you want to get started. In this chapter, we explore the most common financing solutions that you can consider if you want to start your own glamping business.

BENEFITS OF DEBT FINANCING

Securing finance for your glamping business is the very first step to success. There are many initial expenses that you have to cover - and let's face it; we don't all have thousands lying in a bank account. Whether you need to find full funding for your glamping business or only to supplement the savings you already have, there are various types of financial solutions that you can look at.

Debt financing is generally the most common kind of option that people turn to. This relates to applying for a loan in order to finance the glamping business that you want to start. Since you are only starting out with a glamping business, however, it is important to understand that you are unlikely to obtain corporate financing at the time. This is why you will likely need to utilize your own credit record in order to assist with the financing process.

There are several advantages to using debt financing as a solution to getting your glamping business off the ground:

- When you take out a loan to start the business, it means you have ownership of the glampsite. This also means you do not have to constantly report to other people, such as a board of directors or investors before you can make any decision within the business.
- Depending on the type of loan you decide to apply for, you might be able to secure fixed payments. This means you know exactly how much you need to repay the loan every month. It makes the process of setting up a budget for your business significantly easier.

Problems With Debt Financing

There are numerous benefits to expect when you decide to go for debt financing, but you also need to understand the challenges that you may face along the way. This can help you be more realistic about the process and know what to expect.

When you use debt financing, you'll often have trouble finding a lender who shares the same vision related to glamping as you do. Even when you apply for a personal loan and specify the structuring of a glamping site in the process, it can still be difficult to get a lender that is willing to take the risk. There are also times when one lender might not be able to help you with a sufficient amount of funds. In this case, you will need to contact and approach multiple lenders in order to secure all of the capital you need to get started.

Sometimes, a lender might be willing to help you, but only if you are able to provide a personal guarantee. This usually comes in the form of collateral, such as putting up certain assets you own. It is a form of secure financing that allows the bank or another type of financial institution to recover assets from you in the event that you are unable to repay the monthly installments as agreed upon in the contract you sign.

Due to the large amount of money you require, you might need to put assets like your home or car on the line. If things go wrong or not as you planned with the glamping site, then you risk losing the collateral that you put up as a personal guarantee.

Where To Apply For Financing

You have a number of options to consider when you need debt financing for your glamping business. The first option is to consider federal associations that provide assistance to small businesses in the local region. For example, both the USDA and the SBA are departments in the government within the United States that sometimes offer assistance. There are also credit unions that you can contact, as they might also be able to provide you with the financial assistance you require for your business. It is, however, important to understand the specific financing options that are available. Weigh them against each other to find what will work best for your glamping business.

Equity Financing

One of the most popular options that people use when they wish to turn to finance as a way to obtain the funds they need for a glamping business is equity financing. This type of financing does give up a percentage of your business as owner-ship for those who put down funds. It can, however, be an excellent opportunity in cases where you do not have other options available. Venture capital and private equity firms are both options that you can turn to if you wish to use equity financing. Some people also turn to family members and their friends. When these individuals have funds saved up, they might be willing to provide you with a loan - but, in turn, you will need to provide them with "shares" of your business. These "shares" are provided in the form of ownership percentages.

INVENTORY FINANCING

Another relatively popular option that is also trending in the modern day includes inventory financing. This type of financing will not pay for the land that you wish to purchase, marketing, licensing fees, and other related things. Instead, with inventory finance, you can secure the physical products that will make up your business. This includes domes, tents, and other structures that will provide accommodation to your guests. You will need to find a company that provides inventory financing services. This company will then purchase the inventory you require from an appropriate supplier, and the debt to repay the funds used to purchase these items will fall upon you and your business.

REVENUE SHARING METHOD

The revenue-sharing method is an ideal choice for people who still want control over their glamping site, but are unable to secure the right funds to get started. This particular method utilizes the services provided by companies that are already in the glamping industry. Essentially, the organization you work with will help with the purchase of certain facilities and structures. You then need to sign a contract with the organization for a specified period of time. During this timeframe, the company will collect a percentage of the revenue you generate with the specific structures that they bought. This is a flexible option that also comes with less risk. You also do not take on the debt of loans on your end, as the organization you partner up with will carry these expenses. There are also no upfront costs for these units, and the interest rates are usually very low. You also pay back the company as you are able to, as they usually provide quite flexible terms.

OTHER TYPES OF FINANCE OPTIONS

While we discussed the most common types of debt financing options for glamping businesses, there are additional options that you can also consider. Understanding all of your options will ensure you know what to look at and how to assess the financing services, and give you the ability to make more informed decisions. We are going to take a look at four more financing options that you can explore, which can be good choices if the solutions we previously discussed are not suitable for your business structure.

FINANCE LEASE

Leasing is a viable option for glamping cabins, domes, and other types of accommodation. These are often some of the biggest expenses when you set up this type of business. With finance lease options, another company will essentially purchase the domes and other structures you need to set up your glamping site. You will then pay the company a monthly fee in order to "rent" these structures from them. In most cases, you need to continue with the lease or a certain period of time. If you decide to cancel the contract prior to the specified period, you might be liable for a fine. It is important to note that in most cases when the lease is over and you do not renew the contract, the company will expect you to return these items to them.

Hire Purchase

A hire purchase agreement is quite similar to a finance lease, but there are some important differences that you have to keep in mind. With hire purchase, you will still rent the structures you require on your glamping site from a company. The primary difference is the fact that by the end of the lease period, you will be the owner of these structures. This is why these options generally consist of longer terms in order to ensure the repayments you make can cover the costs of the structures, as well as any interest and fees incurred in the process. Note that with hire purchase, the VAT payable on the structures you require will be charged on the deposit that you make toward the company that buys these items.

Bank Loans

We previously mentioned that sometimes you could use your personal credit record as a way to give your glamping business a kickstart. This is essentially where it comes in. Banks are generally reluctant to the idea of working with a startup business, as there are simply too many risks. Since you have not even set up your glamping site at this point, it means the risks are even greater. If you have good personal credit, however, then you could use this as a method to obtain these funds. Visit your local bank and talk to a consultant about the options that are available to you. It is important to mention to the consultant that you are looking to start a business. If you can present them with your business plan, they might consider this particular factor in the decision-making process. If you can prove to the bank that the business is profitable, then you might be more likely to obtain approval.

GRANT FUNDING

Grant funding is another option that essentially gives you access to some free funding. This funding will not make up the entirety of the funds that you need to start your business, but it can certainly help. You also have to understand that the process to secure grant funding is quite strict and tedious, so you have to go through many steps in order to apply for this type of financial aid. The primary factor here is to show these grant providers that your glamping site will have a positive impact on both the community and economy without a local region. This can be tough to do when you are only starting out, but with some consultation and careful planning, it is possible to set up a complete pitch for these grants. If you are awarded a grant, it will usually provide enough funds to cover around 40% of the expenses you estimate to have with your business's startup.

You should now be able to realize just how important it is to secure financing for your business early on. There are many financing options available, so you need to carefully assess every possibility and make a decision based on what works for you, the business plan you have compiled, and your glamping site.

. . .

Now that you know about the procedures to secure finances for your business, it is time to move forward. In the next chapter, we talk about the purchase of glamping structures, how to go about this entire process, and important considerations that you cannot overlook.

Purchasing Glamping Structures

Around six years ago, Anthony Benacquisto and Paul Schauer decided to start their own business in the glamping industry. To date, the two founders work solely in Michigan to provide specific glamping structures that help site owners offer more facilities for their guests to enjoy.

Dry Camp, the name of their business, is not a glamping site. Instead, they produce special types of double hammocks that are comfortable, easy to set up, and ideal for glamping sites that add that luxurious touch to a classic camping experience. Today, the two make around $2,000 every month, calculating roughly $24,000 every year - only with a single product that they sell in this industry.

As you can see here, structures for people to enjoy at a glamping site are critical to the success of these businesses. While Anthony and Paul monetized the fact that people need sleeping structures for their glamping sites, you are now at a point where you need to consider these structures for your business. You will discover a couple of different glamping sleeping structures in this post and a few considerations to keep in mind with each. The goal of this chapter is to help you understand the process of buying the right structures for your glamping business.

Shopping For Sleeping Structures

When it comes to shopping for sleeping structures that you will set up on your glamping site, it is crucial to keep the environment in mind. Some environments are appropriate for different types of sleeping structures, but this is not always the case. Additionally, when you prefer one structure over another, you may need to do more modifications to the piece of land in order to provide a good fit for the structure.

While you shop for sleeping structures that you will use on your glamping site, you do need to keep in mind a couple of factors:

- Will the structures require grading and alterations to the land's layout? This can lead to excessive expenses and the need to hire power equipment. You may also need to get contractors to help with this process.
- Consider whether you plan on adding factors like electricity and plumbing facilities to the campsite. In this case, you have to ensure the sleeping structures you opt for provide compatibility with these features.

- Carefully assess the maintenance procedure for each of the sleeping structure options that you can consider. Some of these structures require more significant maintenance than others, which also leads to higher costs in the long run.
- Do you want to use these sleeping structures only for specific seasons or throughout the year? If you want to offer a 365-day accommodation system, then how well are the sleeping structures suited to every season?
- Assess the uniqueness of different sleeping structures that you are able to choose from. People often turn to glamping sites that can offer them something "different" and "unique". Structures that are easy to mark and offer people something special are more likely to attract an audience that you desire to have at your glamping site.
- Standing out from the crowd is a highly effective method to thrive in the glamping industry. This is why you should assess the structures that competitors in your local area use. You need to identify your own unique selling point, as this will play a large part in helping to win over customers and thrive among the competition.

The cost of these sleeping structures is another important thing to take into account. The cost per unit generally ranges from around $1,500 and can go up to $250,000 in some cases. Make sure you factor in the cost of each sleeping structure type and compare this to the budget that you have available for your glamping business. Remember that the sleeping structures are not the only expense that you will need to cover, so make sure after purchasing a specific type of structure, you will still have an adequate amount of funds left for other expenses.

Another thing to consider is how easy it is to, later on, expand on the sleeping structures that you choose. As your business grows, you might want to add a few upgrades to these structures in the future. In this case, you do not want to buy new structures due to the incompatibility with upgrades among the existing facilities that you have up.

TENTS

The most common kind of sleeping structure that you will find at glamping sites would certainly be tents. While tents are a common occurrence, it doesn't mean you cannot offer a unique experience for your guests when they sleep in a tent. If you take a closer look at the glamping industry, you'll notice quite a diverse variety of tent options you are able to choose from. This gives you the opportunity to find tents that are unique to your own glamping site - and you have the ability to decorate each to match the theme or aesthetic you wish to create with your business.

Tents are generally easy to set up and are also one of the more cost effective options that you can choose when you pick sleeping structures for a glamping site. The tent itself provides a shell for the accommodation that you offer your guests and allows you to use your own creativity in order to set up an interior that provides that "glamor" effect.

. . .

When you do decide to opt for tents, there are a couple of things to keep in mind:

- The shape and size of the tents you opt for are particularly important. They should comply with the amount of space you have available on the land. Make sure you consider the number of tents you want to set up. There should be a large space between multiple tents, as this gives guests more privacy when they stay over at your glamping site.
- Consider the facilities that you want to make available to your guests. Then, ensure the tents you consider are compatible with these facilities. Special linings at the top side can make the process of laying wires for electricity easier, for example.
- Quality is also a critical matter, as weak-quality materials could lead to wear and tear after only a few stays in the tent. Consider the fabrics that the tent uses and how everything comes together.
- The opening at the front of the tent is another important factor. It should come with an adequate closure that helps to provide protection for the guests at night. At the same time, make sure your guests can easily open up the front region and perhaps a couple of windows to allow air inside the tent.
- Consider when you will open your glamping site to the public during the year. If you will be open throughout the entire year, get four-season tents that can withstand UV exposure, rain, strong winds, and other weather conditions.

Bell Tent

GLAMPING PODS & CABINS

While tents do remain a common sight in glamping sites, the use of glamping pods is quickly gaining traction. Glamping pods and cabins essentially fall within one category and refer to structures that offer luxury facilities but still, fit on open land that incorporates a camping experience.

The major benefit that comes with glamping pods is the fact that they are considered four seasonal structures. This means you can allow your guests to stay on your glamping site throughout the entire year, regardless of the weather. A strong pod structure won't be affected by wind or rain. They also offer protection against sunlight to avoid sunburn among your guests.

· · ·

These pods usually come in the form of a tent-like structure but use wood or other materials in their design. This adds more sturdiness to the structure and can offer a more "home" like feeling for guests when they stay over.

It is also generally easy to add facilities like toilets or even entire bathrooms to glamping pods and cabins. They are also spacious enough to fit other facilities, like electricity and even kitchen equipment. This way, your guests have access to all the essentials they need to enjoy their trip.

While you assess the different glamping pod structures that are available, be sure to keep the following factors in mind:

- Pods need to be four seasonal structures to withstand any type of weather condition. This is why you have to carefully assess the materials that make up these pods. Wood is the default material that most manufacturers use for glamping pods, but there are other options too. If wood is used, it should be treated with a special layer to prevent swelling due to exposure to UV rays and rain.
- Both the layout and space inside these pods contribute to the freedom your guests have when they move around. A proper layout will provide easy access to facilities like a bathroom without getting in the way of your guest.
- Air circulation is important for a glamping pod, particularly due to the enclosed structure. Make sure the pods come with windows in addition to

the main door. The windows need to be easy to open up and close.

- Take note of the shape that these pods come in and determine how suitable they are for the specific piece of land you wish to place them on.

Glamping Pod

Airstream RV

When mobility is something that you need with your glamping business, then you should look at travel-friendly sleeping structures that you can utilize. This is where the range of Airstream RVs comes into the picture. The brand has created a wide selection of RV structures that are mobile and easy to transport. On the inside, these RVs offer access to a diverse range of essential facilities that guests are able to enjoy.

. . .

These are certainly some of the more expensive unit options that you can consider, especially if you need to provide your guests with a large open area to use. On the other hand, you can easily transport these RVs to areas where there is an upcoming festival or event - and in these cases, people are often willing to pay substantial amounts for a glamping experience.

There are both standard travel models and more luxurious coach model options available when you look at Airstream's catalog of RVs. In addition to choosing a specific model, some models are also available in different sizes to better comply with both your own and the guest's requirements.

When you decide to invest in RVs from Airstream, keep the following criteria in mind:

- Budget is definitely an important point that you should not overlook here. Some of the Airstream RVs can go well over $150,000 per unit. There are also more affordable options, such as the Basecamp 16, which comes at a price of less than $50,000. Keep in mind how much you are able to spend per unit before you start to look at the models that are available.
- The amount of space you need to offer your guests is another important element. Some of these RVs can be quite restrictive in terms of space, which can make it difficult for guests to move around. If you only intend on providing access to the

Airstream for sleeping purposes, however, then this is not such a big issue.

- Consider additional facilities that come with each of these Airstreams and what your guests will require. Some of the airstreams on the market come with built-in kitchen facilities and sometimes even a bathroom. There are also certain options that come pre-fitted with a bed and a sofa. These facilities add extra comfort elements to the RV.

Airstream RV

YURTS

Yurts are quite similar to tents but take aspects from ancient uses and modernize them. The classic yurt is a type of shelter that ancient civilizations relied on. They were easy to dismantle when needed, which made it easier to take these structures along when communities moved to a different locations. Due to the large size of a yurt's structure, it served as a home for many people.

Today, yurts are becoming quite popular among glamping sites. They come in different shapes and sizes, but the idea remains to use the design of ancient times and turn it into a glamorous structure.

There are several factors that you have to concentrate on when you decide to opt for yurts on your glamping site:

- You first need to inspect the land where you will place the yurts. There should be enough space available. The yurt should also be built upon a flat piece of land. This information will allow you to determine the ideal size for the yurts that you will install on your site. Remember that you will likely install more than just a single yurt, as you will rely on multiple individuals or groups making reservations at your glamping site simultaneously. The yurts should not be spaced too close to each other, as you need to keep the privacy of your guests in mind.
- The shape and layout of the yurt is also an important thing that you should not overlook. Consider any dividers that you need on the interior. These dividers should help to provide private access to facilities like the bathroom and perhaps even a bedroom.
- Consider the facilities you wish to have in the yurt. When you want to provide your guests access to a

bathroom and electricity, then make sure the yurt can accommodate these facilities.

- The structure and frame of the yurt should provide efficient resistance against weather elements. There should not be leaks on the roof when it starts to rain. The materials that make up the roof should also provide efficient resistance against UV rays.
- Consider whether you want the floor of the yurt to extend past its structure. This can add a patio like effect to the structure, which you can add outdoor furniture to. These types of facilities essentially help to improve the overall value of the experience you offer your guests.

Yurt

PREFAB OR TINY HOUSES

Tiny homes have been trending for quite some time now. These homes are compact yet provide people with enough room and the facilities they need for their daily lives. Statistics show that a tiny house accumulates under 20% of the costs associated with buying a normal home. Furthermore, these homes only use an estimated 7% of the electricity a traditional home uses. This correlates to the fact that over half of the people who own a tiny home have no credit card debt.

Tiny homes are not only great as a house to live in but can also make a great choice for a glamping site. You would essentially provide your guests with a full "at home" experience away from their own homes. These homes come in several different shapes, layouts, and sizes. Some are basic and others may even have multiple stories, which adds to the amount of space you can offer your guests inside these tiny homes.

The great thing about tiny houses is the fact that they are generally affordable, and you have the freedom to customize them according to your preferences. This gives you the ability to offer different experiences to guests who come to your glamping site. For example, you could choose a few generic options that are exactly the same and add one or two "luxury" units to the site as well. These luxury units would offer more facilities and a bigger space and bring in more income in the process.

If you are interested in using tiny homes as the accommodation options at your glamping site, then be sure to keep the following tips in mind:

- The idea of a tiny home is to pack several essential facilities into a compact structure. This can sometimes make the person who lives inside the home feel a bit restricted in terms of space. This is why you should first consider the amount of space that each of these tiny home options offers you. Luckily, you can usually have tiny homes designed according to your own plans. Make sure there is enough space in the home for the facilities you will offer access to, as well as for the guests to move around.
- Consider whether you want fixed tiny homes or rather ones that are mobile. A mobile solution will come with a series of wheels attached to the bottom of the frame. This allows you to hook the tiny home up to your vehicle and move it around on your glamping grounds.
- Take note of the materials that you prefer to use for the construction of these homes. Make sure the materials are able to effectively withstand any weather conditions. The materials should also be durable and produce an efficient insulated effect inside the tiny home.

Prefab Cabins

This chapter focused entirely on helping you understand how to go about deciding on the right sleeping structures for your glamping business. We assessed the possibility of using tents, tiny homes, yurts, and several other structures to provide a glamorous accommodation option for your guests.

You now have the ability to determine what type of structures to buy, so the next step of the process is to start setting up the glamping site. In the next chapter, you will discover some of the most important steps that you should take when you want to set up your glampsite. I'll walk you through the essential furniture pieces and facilities to add, as well as show you how the addition of extra amenities can increase the value of your glampsite.

SETTING UP YOUR GLAMPSITE

I n 2015, Katrina and Steve Boydon decided to move back to the area they came from in English Welsh after remaining employed in the United States for a period of two decades. The couple came back to their roots with the idea of opening a glampsite, but first used temporary accommodation while seeking out the perfect spot.

The couple decided to move into the Tanycoed Farm in April 2015, with a land large enough to set up a glamping site and expand on it as they go. In June 2015, the couple was able to open up Barnutopia to the public and started to receive their first guests. Barnutopia is located in the western region of Shropshire and also offers standard camping options, as well as an event venue now. There are currently seven glamping sites that guests can book, with an eighth one coming soon.

The success of Barnutopia is largely due to the excellent marketing procedures that the couple have implemented to promote their business, but also due to the unique take they have on accommodation options and amenities that are available to guests.

When it comes to succeeding with your glamping business, simply placing the structures that offer accommodation to guests on the land is not enough. You need to carefully plan everything out from the start. Add the right facilities and amenities, and make sure guests feel comfortable with the furniture they gain access to in the sleeping structures.

The details that I share with you in this chapter will help you better understand the setup of a glamping site. You will discover how you should plan for the layout and the importance of certain facilities on the land. The chapter will also provide details about the most important furniture pieces that you should add to the glamping structures that guests will stay in. You can also identify the most helpful amenities that can add value to your site and essentially help you bring in more money in the process.

FACILITIES TO ADD

You already know about the specific tents that you are going to use for your business, so now it is time to consider the facilities you wish to offer your guests. An ideal glamping experience would include facilities such as showers, a toilet that is easy to use, and a stove inside the accommodation. Of course, the facilities you add largely depend on the budget you have and the type of glamping experience you wish to add to your site.

. . .

For example, many glamping sites offer their guests access to Wi-Fi internet, but this is not a necessity. You can decide to offer an experience that allows your guests to break away from technology and rather enjoy mother nature. This type of experience does not call for on-site Wi-Fi access.

Most glamping sites will, however, at least need to give their guests access to clean water. This means you will need to get a local contractor to lie pipes and provide plumbing services to the glamping structures that you set up. While installing plumbing systems, consider how you will provide access to toilets. If you decide to add a shower and sink to the units, then make sure the plumber completes these plumbing systems during this process too.

Electricity is another facility that you should consider adding to your glamping site. This is something that has become quite a standard among glamping businesses and also a facility that guests may expect to find at your site. Again, you will need to get a professional electrician to lay the electrical lines in such a way that they offer power to each of the units on your property.

When you decide to add a facility such as a camp stove in the glamping structures, then keep your guest's safety in mind. Add a fire extinguisher to every unit to ensure fires can be put out quickly in unforeseen cases.

Outdoor Shower

ESSENTIAL FURNITURE

When it comes to setting up the units that will provide accommodation for your guests, you have to focus on furnishing each one properly. This includes adding a few essential pieces of furniture that guests generally rely on first. Furniture is really what completes that "glamor camping" experience for the people who will visit your site. Without the right furniture pieces, you may find that guests feel that the site offers them more of a traditional camping experience than glamping.

Many people will use glamping as an opportunity to explore nature, which means some may mainly focus on the glamping structures you set up as a way to sleep at night. This is why it is important to start with the beds that you add to these units. You should ensure you buy comfortable beds that your guests can enjoy sleeping on. This will help to add to that "luxury" experience they expect from a glamping site.

Once you have the right beds in mind, consider blankets and pillows too. This is where aesthetics start to come into play. You need to decide what decorative themes or elements you want to have at your glamping site - and then focus on these factors while you shop for different furniture and decor items.

Make a list of colors or compile a few pictures that you can refer to for the style that you want to establish.

The bedding items that you buy, including the sheets and pillowcases, should provide a match for this style. It is a good idea to cultivate the same decor among each of the units. You can, however, add some alterations to the aesthetics you want to maintain in some of your luxury units. This can make them more attractive to customers who are able to pay more for their night's stay.

Apart from a bed and linen, here are other things that you should also focus on when you get the essential furniture:

- Add bedside tables to the area where the bed stands. If it is a single bed, add only a single bedside table. You need a bedside table on both sides of the beds if you add a double or larger bed to the structure. It is also a good idea to add lamps on these tables. This offers easy access to lighting when the guests sleep.

- A couple of chairs are also a good idea in cases where you have sufficient space in the structures you set up on your glamping site. For added comfort, some glamping site owners add a sofa to the interior of these structures. If you have a structure with a small patio, then you can also consider the addition of chairs outside. Make sure these chairs are weatherproof.

- Lights in the glamping structure are also an essential piece that you should take care of. This ensures the guests feel comfortable at night when they decide to go into their unit and spend the rest of the evening there. If you decide not to add electricity to your glamping site, then set up lights that rely on batteries.

- Add a rug to the area. This helps to prevent the interior of the unit from becoming too cold and can also easily contribute to the decor in the area.

- People who stay at a glamping site for a while may also request a wardrobe. Install this early on to avoid problems when guests want to hang up a few pieces of clothing. Be sure to add some hangers to each of these wardrobes.

- It is a good idea to add a mirror to the interior of each unit too. Try to aim for a relatively large mirror that offers adequate guest coverage. Many guests may want to apply makeup, do their hair, or simply ensure their outfit seems fine before they exit the unit in the morning.

- To add extra convenience to your glamping structures, consider adding a desk or table. This can be used when the guests dine or to enjoy a few games with the family. A desk also adds some extra storage space that your guests can use to keep their personal belongings.

- A stove is another crucial facility that some people may demand in a glamping site, but it is not essential. You can choose to rather add campfires outside with appropriate equipment to have a barbecue. This can help to cultivate that classic camping experience while still offering luxury accommodations.

- Consider adding a shower that has access to hot water for your guests. This further adds to the glamping experience and allows them to feel clean and refreshed.

Apart from these facilities, it is important to prioritize the safety of the guests who decide to stay at your glamping site. The most basic factor that you can add to improve the safety of every guest is a series of locks. Make sure every unit on the property you own or rent has a different lock that is used for the front door. This ensures that each key only works on a specific glamping structure and not the other ones. Make sure the windows can also lock when the guest closes them. If there are large windows, be sure to add some curtains to them, as this also helps to provide a better level of privacy.

In terms of security, you can consider adding emergency buttons to each of the units on your glamping site. Have this button send a signal to your security guards or to the main office. This way, guests will have peace of mind knowing that they can gain access to security services if something should happen.

Essential Furniture

EXTRA AMENITIES

You now have a good view of the most essential furniture and facilities that you need to implement for your guests. Once these are taken care of, the next step is to add more value to your glamping units. When you decide to add extra amenities to your glamping units, it also means you are able to charge your guests more for their stays. In turn, this helps to push up the revenue you can see come into your business.

Of course, there is no need to start off with all the extra amenities that we are going to discuss. You can start out with the basics when you first open your glamping business to the public. As your business grows, you can then gradually start to add additional amenities and facilities to make the lives of your guests more comfortable and convenient.

We will discuss a couple of extra amenities that you should consider adding to your glamping structures below:

- Decorations are particularly important when it comes to setting up your glamping structures. You need to add that extra "glamor" to these structures - apart from the beds, showers, stoves, and sofas. There are many different kinds of decorations that you can choose to add, but it does come down to the specific aesthetics you wish to add to your glamping site. You could add some fairy lights and a few portraits to each unit, for example.
- It's a good idea to offer each guest a "welcome pack" as an extra amenity. This pack could include some sticks and marshmallows, as well as a few recipes that they can try on the campfires that you have set up close to the accommodation. If you offer guests access to Wi-Fi, then add a card to this pack that provides them with the password and details about how they can get connected.
- A patio heater is also a good idea, especially during winter months. This can help to ensure the guests can enjoy the patio and the outdoor view of nature without getting too cold.
- If you have a large open field that people can use when they visit your glamping site, then consider offering foldable picnic tables. You can also offer guests access to picnic baskets and a blanket that they can use outdoors.

- Adding a few board games to each of the units on your glampsite is another great idea. This can add some entertainment to keep your guests busy and gives them an opportunity to move away from their phones and rather spend quality time with each other.

- Coffee is one of the most popular hot beverages that people enjoy - and many people can't start the day without a cup. This is why it is also a great idea to add a coffee machine to these units. This is definitely a luxury element that will instantly add value to your glamping site. There is no need to purchase expensive coffee machines. Even manual options alongside a kettle can work. Add a few samples of coffee next to the amenity, as this gives people the ability to enjoy coffee without having to bring their own ground or beans.

- A laundry room on site is another great idea that you should look into. This type of service is especially useful for guests who will stay at your site for a couple of days. They will have dirty clothes that they want to clean, which is where a laundry room or service comes in.

Other than these amenities, you should also consider offering the option to add an outdoor pizza oven to these units and provide your guests with hammocks. Offering some mystical fire powder for your guests can also add some fun to their time around the campfire at night.

Extra Amenities

FURNISH SMART

It's important to be smart when you shop for furniture and the structures that you are going to offer as accommodation on your glamping site. This is where prioritization comes into the picture. By prioritizing your purchasing process, it is easier to ensure you spend the right amount of money on each element. Remember that the overall appearance and comfort that your structures offer guests will have a major impact on how much you can charge per night. For example, the right furnishings can be the main difference between the ability to charge $50 or $300 for a single night's stay.

Comfort is the top priority that you need to focus on when you decide to set up a glamping site. Thus, spend more on the items that are going to make your guests feel comfortable. This starts with the tent or other structure that you decide to opt for, followed by things like the mattress and foundation that your guests will sleep on. It's better to spend more here and then turn to stores that offer decorations at discounted prices. You can even turn to vintage stores to add a rustic feel to your glamping structures - this is a great way to save money when decorating while still adding a stylish aesthetic element to your glampsite.

You should now have a good idea about how you can go about setting up your glampsite. I talked about the important role that essential furniture plays and how you should prioritize your shopping when you set out a budget. Do not be cheap when it comes to factors that contribute to the comfort of your guests - as these factors contribute to their overall experience. Add extra amenities to create a more valuable experience for each guest that decides to book a night at your glamping site.

Now that you know how to set up your glamping site, it is important to start looking at ways in which you can promote your business. The next chapter is all about listing your business at appropriate directories and setting up marketing strategies to get your glamping site noticed. I will walk you through factors like setting up a website for your business, creating social media profiles, and more.

LISTING ON AIRBNB
AND PROMOTING YOUR
BUSINESS

At the start of the previous chapter, we looked at how Barnutopia went from idea to reality. We also considered the important role that choosing the right setup for their business played. Now, I want to look quickly at how they used marketing to get their name out there.

The owners announced that Facebook has been playing a major role in helping with the growth of the business ever since the start. In fact, the majority of visitors come from Facebook, but they also largely depend on other marketing strategies to promote Barnutopia. The company also has a website now, which provides an easy way for customers to make bookings. Again, Barnutopia's owners report Facebook as an important source of traffic for their website as well. Search engine optimization has also allowed the company's website to rank and bring in organic traffic.

. . .

This goes to show just how important advertising and promotion of a glamping business is. When people do not know about your glamping site after you open it up to the public, then you won't receive any bookings. Sure, some people do rely on factors like word-of-mouth marketing - but this isn't something that you can depend on when you only start out. Instead, you will need to set up a proper marketing plan to ensure people can easily find your business.

This is also where the internet comes into play. The internet has made it exceptionally easy for people to find exactly what they are looking for - and that includes glamping sites that they can use to unwind and enjoy a glamorous camping experience. So, take advantage of this by ensuring you get your business up on the internet and make it easy for people to find it.

This chapter focuses on a diverse range of marketing techniques that you are able to rely on when you have your glamping business up and running. We look at the role that your website, digital marketing strategies, and social media management plays. We also consider the potential that listing on certain websites can have for your business.

How To Advertise Your Glampsite

Learning how to advertise your glampsite is crucial. The main problem here is that many people who want to start their own glamping business do not have the expertise to promote their business. Hiring an agency is surely a possible option, but when you are working with a tight budget, learning to do things yourself is generally a good idea. You should ensure you learn about the basics of marketing and start to implement a solid strategy before you open up your doors to the public. This can help to cultivate some initial interest in your business - ensuring you already have bookings by the time you allow guests to stay at your glamping site.

There are several techniques that you can use when you promote your business. Many people do, however, search on the internet when they want to find a good glamping site to visit. This is why you should focus on creating listings for your website and ensure you set up a business profile on Google. These initial elements can go a long way in improving the exposure you are able to obtain for your glamping site.

You can still rely on some conventional local advertising options, such as setting up posters at your local supermarket. There are also newspaper entries and advertisements in magazines that you can consider, but they are nowadays more costly compared to digital promotions.

BUSINESS WEBSITE

An online presence is important for any modern-day business, regardless of industry, what you offer, and how big of a company you have. Even small and local companies now establish an online presence for themselves, as this helps them reach a wider audience.

This is why a good first step that you should take includes setting up an official business website for your glamping site. This website will serve many purposes. It provides a hub that customers can land on when they search for glamping spots in the area. The website can also provide a showcase of what customers can expect if they choose to make a booking. Additionally, with some plugins and tools, you can also integrate a booking system onto your website, which makes it easy to get bookings and keep things organized.

There are a couple of options that you can explore when it comes to setting up a website. The first step, however, is to choose and register a domain name. You can use local domain extensions, but many companies rely on .com extensions due to their global reach. Choose a domain name that effectively represents your glamping site's name, as this makes it more memorable for the customer. For example, if your glamping site's name is "Farm Glamping", then choose a domain like "farmglamping.com". In addition to the domain name, you will also need to find a hosting provider that will host your website. It's definitely a good idea to use the same provider for both the hosting and your domain name. This ensures you get all your bills on a single platform for easier management.

Once you have hosting up and you registered your domain name, the next step is the website. Now, there are two ways that you can go about setting up a website to represent your company:

1. The first and probably easiest step is to hire a professional freelancer or an agency that specializes in website development. This can, however, incur a lot of charges, so make sure you take a closer look at your budget at this point. These professionals

can use their expertise and experience to set up a great-looking website on your behalf. You can then get these pros to also manage your website and perform regular maintenance, as well as updates. Note that you will also need to pay for the continuous maintenance that they will provide.

2. The second option is to go the DIY route. With content management systems like WordPress, the process of setting up a website has become much easier than in the past. You don't even have to write a single line of code to get a great-looking website up for your glamping business. Some hosting providers may provide assistance services, such as the option to have WordPress installed on your server. Then, choose a theme, add a few plugins, and set up the content of each page.

If you do not have enough budget left to hire professionals, then take a look at a few video tutorials on how WordPress works. There are also alternative content management systems, such as Joomla and Drupal, that also offer a no-code experience when you set up a website. You also get to explore a diverse selection of both paid and free themes, which instantly changes the appearance of your website. Take advantage of this to find a theme that effectively represents the look and feel you want to establish for your glamping site. Make sure you cover all of the important aspects, such as a great homepage, an about us page, and a page where customers can contact you from. A gallery or showcase page is also important and should provide an overview of the best things you have to offer at your glamping site.

Google Business Listing

Once you have your website up and running, an important step that many people often overlook is to set up a Google Business Listing. Google still remains one of the world's most popular search engines, and people use it not only to find information online but also to locate and discover businesses. An estimated 92.05% of people who use a search engine on the internet will turn to Google instead of other search engines.

The Google Business system has provided a significant range of benefits for businesses that want to promote themselves on the internet. If you search for a business online, you will often see a side block pop up on the right of the screen with business information. You can also click to find more businesses on a map. These are all Google Business profiles that you can view - and you should aim to get your business listed there too.

You do need a Google account to do this, but if you have a Gmail email address, then you already have this type of account. Simply sign into Google My Business and choose to add a new business under your account. Here, you should upload photos of your glampsite and provide relevant information. Try to be as detailed as possible, as this can help to ensure people are able to easily find your company on the internet. You also have to ensure you link your Google My Business listing to your website, as this can help to drive extra traffic to your online property.

Regularly check back on your profile to look for reviews, and be sure to respond to them. It is also important to update your profile if anything changes and to add new photos from time to time.

LISTING ON AIRBNB & OTHER OTAS

Maximizing the exposure of your business is crucial, so be sure to take advantage of OTA platforms. These platforms focus on helping travelers find accommodation wherever they go. It is an excellent opportunity to increase the number of bookings you get, and most of these platforms have a relatively low service fee. The great thing here is that you pay a service fee but do not have to worry too much about advertising your glamping site on the app or website. Once you are listed, people can easily find your glampsite when they search for glamping experiences in the area you are located.

TOP OTAS TO LIST YOUR PROPERTIES ON

There are a variety of OTAs and other listing websites that you can use to promote your business. It is important to note, however, that the regulations and fees differ among the platform options that you are able to utilize. This is why it is so important to carefully understand the importance of filtering through the listing platforms and choosing ones that comply with your needs.

LISTING ON AIRBNB

Airbnb has been around for quite some time now, but experienced a decline in 2020. Following this setback, the company was quickly able to recover from the setback, seeing a 280.2% increase in income just the next year. In August 2022, Airbnb was valued at around $70 billion. There are now more than four million hosts that rely on Airbnb to help them bring in extra income by offering vacation rentals. In just the second quarter of 2022, Airbnb's platform received over 100 million bookings for experiences and stays. To date, more than one billion bookings have been made on the platform.

Why show you these statistics? Because it's direct evidence that Airbnb is a winner - a platform that helps millions of people make extra money by renting out space that they have. One thing that people sometimes misunderstand about Airbnb is the fact that it is a platform for more than just the average homeowner looking to rent out a room or a cottage in the backyard.

Airbnb has grown into a full accommodation system that even resorts, hotels, and - of course - glamping site owners rely on. It's not that hard to get listed on the platform and they keep fees relatively low, which allows you to still profit when Airbnb is able to send you bookings for your glamping site.

You do need to ensure you have everything up and running before you register at Airbnb. There are also certain verification processes that you need to go through before your listing will be approved. When you collect everything you need prior to setting up the listing, then things will be easier during the registration process.

There are many benefits that you get when you decide to list with Airbnb. They take privacy and protection seriously, so here are just a few of these important features:

- Guest identity verification to ensure the guests who arrive at your glamping site are who they say they are, and trustworthy.
- Reservation screening service.
- Up to $3 million in damage protection against art, valuables, automobiles, boats, pets, and your income.
- Airbnb hosts also get access to a $1 million liability insurance service.
- There is a 24-hour safety line hosts can access.

In terms of fees, Airbnb has competitive rates that are actually quite convenient. The great thing about the service offered at Airbnb is the fact that the fees they charge are essentially split between you and your guests. When someone makes a booking to stay at your glamping site, Airbnb will automatically charge them a booking fee, in addition to collecting the funds required for the bookings they make. On your end, you will usually pay a flat service fee that is equivalent to 3% of the total that the customer pays for the booking. These are generally the only fees involved with the process.

Additionally, when you go a bit out of your way to make guests feel welcome, you can easily start to rake in positive reviews. Positive reviews are essential for maintaining your listing on Airbnb and also makes it more likely for guests to book a unit and an experience at your glamping site. Over time, there is also the opportunity to become what is known as a "superhost". This gives you access to a range of additional benefits, but you will have to work your way up there.

List on Airbnb!

OTHER OTAS TO LIST ON

While Airbnb is a great choice for people with a glamping site who wants to expand their exposure, do not only limit yourself to this OTA platform. There are several other websites that are also excellent for attracting customers who are interested in having a glamping experience. We will take a closer look at a few of the other OTA platforms that you should also list on and not overlook below:

- **Glamping Hub:** Glamping hub is dedicated to hosts who are in the industry. The platform also focuses on helping people who want a luxury camping experience find a site in the area they want to travel to. There are over 19,000 campsites on the hub already and they continue to expand. There are no listing fees that you have to pay and you get global exposure if you decide to list your glampsite on this website. Furthermore, there are also no contracts or commitments that you have to undertake, which means you can cancel your listing on the Glamping Hub at any time and without any notice. Glamping Hub also regularly shares experiences and tips that educate customers, which attracts more users - and helps to add more exposure for the listings on the website.

- **The Dyrt:** The primary idea behind The Dyrt platform is to provide a central hub for people who enjoy camping. The company offers a wide range of camping resources, including useful maps that people can rely on when they want to go hiking. In addition to standard camping grounds and sites, there are also listings that focus on glamping companies. This makes it an excellent opportunity for you to further add to the exposure you can get for your glamping business. This platform offers a commission-free booking service and the website receives around 27 million visitors every year. The instant booking feature also helps to make it easier for customers to book a room on your site.

- **Pitchup:** If you decide to open up your glamping site in the United States, United Kingdom, or within Europe, then you definitely have to list on Pitchup too. The website has a five-star service rating on Feefo with over 100,000 current reviews. Customers are given the opportunity to choose from a diverse range of different camping sites - including glamping structures. The company behind Pitchup has won several awards and has been featured in The Daily Telegraph, The

Guardian, The Sun, and several other news
publications.

- **Hipcamp:** Hipcamp is all about helping people
  experience the great outdoors. At Hipcamp,
  people can search for a variety of different
  camping experiences, such as regular campsites or
  more luxurious options like your glamping site.
  Hipcamp has a 4.5 star rating on Trustpilot with
  well over 5,000 reviews at the moment. The great
  thing about this website is that they divide their
  glamping listings into several categories. This can
  help to maximize your exposure among people
  looking to visit a glamping site with the specific
  sleeping structures, extra amenities, or specific
  properties that you are able to offer them.

List For Success

You now have a good view of important platforms to get your
glamping site listed on, but simply drafting up something
basic is not going to lead to success. You have to carefully plan
out how you will list your business in order to make it more
appealing to those individuals who land on the page.

In this section, I am going to discuss a couple of useful tips
that can help you set up a better listing for your glamping
business. These details will help you better understand what
you should do in order to maximize the exposure of each
listing you set up. While you assess these, note that it is a good
idea to change a few things a bit from each other when you list
on different websites. This can make it seem less like a copy
and paste job and may also help with rankings.

- Put an emphasis on the unique selling point of your business.
- Make sure you take high quality and professional photos, then post them on your listings.
- Change the photos on your page according to the current season.
- Outline the advantages that your sleeping structures offer for the current season.
- Regularly update the contents and information.
- Provide a full range of rules and regulations that you implement on the campsite.
- Use software to manage any bookings you get from these websites. This allows you to have everything synced into a single system to avoid confusion or overbooking.
- Make listings for each of the units that you have available.

In addition to these factors, make sure you regularly check for messages and feedback. Listen to any feedback that customers offer and reply to reviews.

Social Media

Millions of people use platforms like Facebook, TikTok, Twitter, and Instagram. These social media platforms allow people to keep in touch with their friends and remain entertained at the same time. With the vast adoption of social media platforms, it is important to target these networks with your marketing campaigns too.

· · ·

Set up a Facebook page that represents your business, as well as an account on TikTok, Instagram, and Twitter. You can use tools like Hootsuite to automate the process of posting content to these channels. With TikTok, take advantage of the short videos by showing sights on your glamping site. When you have everything set up, take advantage of TikTok Now, Instagram Reels, and Facebook Stories to further expand your ability to reach your audience.

You should now have a good understanding of the role that marketing and listings play in the process of promoting your glamping business. Make sure you follow through on each of the topics we discussed. This allows you to have a website to represent your glamping business, as well as a social media presence.

Now that we have covered these factors, it is time to look at how you should go about the management and maintenance of your glamping business in the next chapter. We will consider the specific ongoing things you should do to guarantee the success of your glamping site.

MANAGING AND MAINTAINING A GLAMPING BUSINESS

The management of a glamping site is imperative. You need to understand the specific methods involved in the process of maintaining the glampsite after the initial opening - and the maintenance really starts the moment you open your site to the public.

Examples we can look at come from Greece, where the two prominent glamping sites at the moment are able to continue thriving. Vasilikia Mounted Resort, located a short drive from Pavliani, is situated at the entrance to the popular Oti National Park. By choosing the right location, this glamping site is capable of attracting a significant number of visitors.It is, however, due to the excellent management skills from the owners of the glamping site that the business is able to continue thriving after several years.

This is just one example that shows proper management can lead to years or even centuries of success. One of the main problems, however, is that many people who decide to set up a glamping business do not have extensive management experience. Even if you do have experience in management, it might not be related to the rental or tourism industry - which means there are still some things that you need to learn in the process.

This chapter entirely focuses on the process of both managing your glamping business once you open it up, as well as the maintenance steps you need to implement. Management essentially ensures you do not do overbookings and can provide your customers with invoices and quotations, while also keeping your books in check. Maintenance will have a direct impact on customer satisfaction, as it ensures the sleeping structures are kept clean and the land remains in a great condition over time.

Rental Property Maintenance

Maintenance plays a key role in the management of any rental property. This includes apartments that you rent out, and even the sleeping structures that you offer as temporary residence while people want to enjoy their glamping trip. Since you are renting out this space, it falls onto you to ensure the environment remains clean. When you fail to thoroughly clean a glamping structure before new guests arrive, it could leave them feeling disgusted with your site. This can also lead to hygiene related hazards and problems, which could essentially turn into legal matters in some cases.

There are several steps involved with the maintenance of your glamping site. It is important that you take care of each step in order to avoid unhappy customers or expose your guests to certain hazards.

In this section, I am going to tell you more about why you have to implement a maintenance plan, the costs you will need to cover, and a couple of other important matters.

Why Is Vacation Rental Maintenance So Important?

Let's start by considering why it is so important to have a maintenance plan for your glamping business. Note that maintenance does not necessarily refer to having a cleaning team that can clean out the glamping structures every time a guest leaves. It rather provides a view at a bigger picture - and could end up saving you a lot in the long run.

When you implement maintenance processes, you usually get a construction worker to inspect the buildings on your property. They can then identify any potential faults with the buildings in general and fix them before these problems become larger concerns. When issues are fixed early on, then they won't develop further. For example, if there is a crack in a wooden board that makes up the exterior shell on one of your structures, it could worsen over time. This may eventually lead to the need to replace multiple planks that make up the exterior shell of the unit. If you implemented a maintenance plan on a regular basis, then a contractor would have noted the crack. At this time, the crack might simply need some filler or basic repair work - and this would prevent it from causing further harm to the building's structure.

Apart from saving you funds in the long run, another important benefit that comes with maintenance of your vacation rental properties is the fact that you can keep customers happier. When customers arrive at your glamping site, only to find that the roof of the structure they sleep in starts to leak when it rains - this is sure to ruin the reputation of your site. Customers are very likely to complain about this and may turn to review sites to report the issues they faced.

Thus, proper maintenance can help to avoid problems that will make customers complain and leave bad feedback on your company's online profiles. It will also give the client a more pleasant experience, which makes them more likely to return to your glampsite in the future. Of course, this is also where the valuable word of mouth marketing plays a role. When you impress your guests and there is nothing to complain about, they are also more likely to recommend your glampsite to their friends who want to have a similar experience.

What Maintenance Costs Are Involved?

In a previous chapter, I've touched the topic around the fact that you do not only have initial expenses with a glamping business, but there are also ongoing costs that you have to keep in mind. There is no fixed amount of money that you will incur on a monthly basis for maintenance, as a range of different variables come into play here.

The initial cost would involve the fees that a contractor charges for their services. You do need to ensure you turn to an experienced contractor who is able to provide you with professional services. This may cost a bit more, but it is worth it - as the expertise of the contractor allows them to identify even the smallest issues that could lead to big problems in the future.

. . .

The fees are usually charged per inspection or per hour. Consult with the contractor you choose to understand how they charge you for the services.

Once maintenance is complete, the contractor will provide you with a full report. This report will outline all the checks they performed and offer an overview of any issues detected during the inspection. It is important to consider which of these issues require immediate attention - and then attend to them. If you are not sure, talk to the contractor. The contractor's expertise allows them to help you prioritize the different issues that you need to address on your glampsite.

Any issues that you need to fix will result in extra costs for maintenance. You should get quotations from multiple suppliers when there are items that you need to buy for the process. Get the contractor who inspected your site to provide you a quotation on how much they would charge for services rendered when they fix these problems. Shopping around a bit is a good idea, as this can help you find the best price - not the cheapest, but the most cost effective based on expertise and experience.

Regular maintenance may also sometimes include things like deep cleaning the structures that you allow your guests to stay in, as well as factors like repainting, doing touch ups to certain elements, and more. These are also costs that you will have to carry - but making these expenses now can help to ensure you do not sit with larger expenses later on.

When Should You Perform Routine Maintenance?

It is true that regular maintenance helps to provide you with lower expenses in the long run. While you do need to pay fees to get maintenance done and to attend to any issues that are detected in the process, it does cost you less compared to waiting until a problem escalates into a big concern.

With this in mind, it is important that you consider the ideal frequency at which you should implement these routine maintenance checks. There is no need to have a contractor come out to do a maintenance check too frequently. This can be costly, but you also do not want to wait too long.

It is a good idea to have a checkup done about once or twice a year. If you do a six-month checkup, then it is also a good idea to have some standard routine maintenance tasks implemented at the same time. This may include providing a touchup of any protective layers you apply to the exterior of the units you have on the glampsite, for example.

How To Properly Maintain Your Vacation Rental

Having a checklist on hand is a great way to ensure you take care of all the maintenance steps that are required to uphold your vacation rental units. This also helps you better understand every step of the process and gives you the ability to avoid problems down the line due to improper maintenance.

· · ·

We will discuss the most important factors that are involved in properly maintaining your glamping units below:

- Regular inspections are some of the most crucial tasks that you have to perform. It is a good idea to get a professional in from a third party. This ensures they can perform a thorough inspection on all the units and elements that are available on your property.
- Following these regular inspections, make sure you request a full inspection report from the contractor. Carefully assess the inspection report and decide on any actions you should take at the time to improve your facility and avoid future issues.
- Having a policy in place for your glamping site is critical. This is a form of documentation that provides you with protection against property damage. Make sure you establish rules related to the breakage of items that are available in each of the units you offer as accommodation. Additionally, the policy should also provide details of what happens should a guest result in damage to the glamping structures on your property.
- If there are any special "house rules" that you wish to implement, be sure to describe them in the policy documentation that you set up.
- Send the policy via email to clients when they make a booking and give them a physical copy upon arrival. This can help to promote better adherence to any rules that you want to enforce on your glamping site.

- Make sure you understand your own skills and those of the staff that helps with running the site. If you or some of the staff members have certain skills, you might decide that these skills can be put to use for DIY jobs when needed. This can help to reduce the need for constantly hiring professionals on an as-needed basis to do basic tasks on your property.
- Automating certain factors of your business, including some of the communication, can also be very helpful. Have a system in place that can read reports about maintenance requirements. These systems can automatically send a request for repairs or other services to professionals that you have on your contact list. You can also automate the process of communicating the policy with your customers and answering some common questions that they might have.

Cleaning Checklist

Maintenance is important, sure, but you also have to pay attention to the process of keeping your entire property clean. This does not only include the inside of every unit that is available as a rental, but also the exterior area where guests can roam and enjoy themselves throughout the day. This is where a cleaning checklist comes in handy, as it ensures you are able to effectively delegate tasks to the cleaning staff that you have hired. If you have a large number of units and allow guests to stay throughout the year, then it is a good idea to have on-premise staff members that are responsible for cleaning. This will also lead to lower fees compared to hiring a cleaning company regularly.

Cleaning Your Vacation Rental Property

There are different cleaning methods that you should utilize when it comes to a glamping site. While your guests are staying at the site, it is important to avoid having your staff members get in their way. On the other hand, once the guests leave, it is critical to ensure you perform a deeper clean. This helps to prepare the unit for the next guests that will arrive and stay in the structure.

This is why we will take a closer look at cleaning methods to use throughout the entire rental process - both during the time when your guests stay in a unit and afterward once they leave. While considering these factors, it is important to understand how long it takes your staff members to thoroughly clean a glamping structure after the guests sign out at your facility. Keep this in mind when you make bookings, as you do not want to have new guests arriving before the staff is able to completely clean the unit.

Cleaning During Your Guests' Stay

The most difficult part here is often during the period when the guest stays at your glamping site. Some guests may not be comfortable allowing cleaning staff into the unit in order to clean. They may have concerns related to the safety of the belongings they have or feel that it interferes with their privacy.

The best solution here is to ask the guest if they would like to have their unit cleaned during their stay. Some guests may prefer to clean up after themselves. You can add a clause in the policy that asks guests to at least clean up any messes they make in the unit prior to their departure. If the guest requests to keep the unit clean themselves, then you will simply not dispatch your cleaning staff to these particular structures while the guests are staying there.

On the other hand, should the guests request cleaning services during their stay, then you should ask them what the most appropriate times are for your staff to clean their unit. Make sure you set up a proper schedule for your staff members to ensure they know which unit to clean at specific times throughout the day. This can help to reduce the risk of confusion between staff members and the guests who are staying at your glamping site.

Make sure you consider any specific allergies that your guests may have to ingredients used in common cleaning detergents. You should avoid using any products that could potentially result in an allergic reaction or other sensitivity reactions among your guests.

CLEANING AFTER YOUR GUESTS LEAVE

Things are generally easier when your guests have already booked out and left the premises. You can send a team of cleaners into the unit, and they can work together to clean things up. A deeper cleaning is definitely required once your guest leaves, as you are now preparing the unit for the arrival of the next guests. If you do not have an inventory of extra bedding, then you should now ensure the staff washes the pillowcases, pillows, and blankets that you supplied on the bed within the unit.

. . .

Deep cleaning involves properly dusting off the entire area. The staff should also ensure they properly clean the floors and look for any stains on the walls within the unit. These should also be attended to at this point. Make sure the staff cleans up any papers, wrappers, bottles, or other items that the recent guests might have forgotten to pick up and throw away. Cleaning the curtains and using a vacuum on the mattress and other furniture pieces in the unit is also useful.

In cases where you have a stove in these units, you should also ensure any cookware you offer alongside this amenity is cleaned thoroughly, then packed back into the appropriate storage system you have in the glamping structure.

Once cleaning is done, make sure everything looks tidy and remember to add the welcome pack you offer your guests before you lock the door. In addition to cleaning the interior, make sure your staff also attends to the outside area. Pick up any trash, clean the patio if applicable, and make sure there is no leftover ash in the campfire site that you offer the guests access to. A clean environment is definitely a benefit for the next guests who arrive at your glamping site.

Vacation Rental Cleaning Checklist

When you have to ensure your staff cleans multiple units clean, especially before new guests arrive, the process can quickly start to feel daunting. This is why you should have a planning system on hand - and a checklist is definitely something to keep nearby too.

. . .

A vacation rental cleaning checklist essentially gives you a list of ticks that you can look at when you inspect a glamping unit before new guests book in. You can go from top to bottom on these lists in order to identify any areas that are not properly cleaned and might be noticeable by your guests.

Here are some things that you should consider adding to your glamping unit cleaning checklist:

- Outside campfire - ash and wood removed, container cleaned.
- Patio - make sure the patio is properly cleaned, and any stains are removed.
- Pick up any litter that you notice outside the unit.
- Remove linen from beds and send it to the laundry.
- Vacuum and mop the floors on the interior of the unit.
- Vacuum the top side of the mattress and make sure there are no stains.
- Clean sofas and other furniture pieces in the unit.
- Clean any outdoor furniture that you offer with the unit.
- Clean any cutlery, cookware, and utensils that come with the rental of the glamping structure.
- Replace sugar, coffee, and other perishable items that you add for the convenience of your guests.

This list provides an excellent starting point to get you going with a checklist. Make sure you create a checklist with tick boxes. This can help you mark the cleaning tasks as you go - and reduce the risk of skipping a task that ends up being important.

In addition to this checklist, you should also regularly do inventory of the cleaning items and products you use. Keep a checklist of the detergents and make sure you always have sufficient stock of each.

MANAGING DIFFICULT GUESTS AND RESPONDING TO BAD REVIEWS

Regardless of the industry you are in; you will eventually have to deal with difficult customers. This especially accounts for the hospitality and rental industries. How you manage these difficult guests will have a big impact on how it impacts your business in general. When you do not remain calm during a conflict with a guest, it could cause problems for you - and this can give your business a bad reputation. It is important to note that while positive reviews are great for your business, many people looking for a glamping site will first start by reading through the bad reviews that people have left. When you have a difficult guest that feels unsatisfied with a resolution you came up with, they will likely rant on the internet when they leave a review for your glamping site.

This is bad for business and something that you want to avoid. Equipping yourself with the knowledge to not only manage difficult guests but also to identify different types of customers is important. Do this early on, and you will surely be able to tell an easy customer from a difficult one. This way, you can change the way you interact with customers based on their typc - and this can sometimes save you from having to face unpleasant situations and getting those bad reviews that have a negative impact on your company's reputation.

In this section, we are going to look at a few signs that show a customer might be a difficult one. Being able to notify your staff to be careful can help to make things go smoother when you have a difficult guest staying at your glamping site. I am also going to note a few safety procedures that I highly recommend you take advantage of. These procedures can help you manage certain events that may come up while you need to deal with these difficult guests.

IDENTIFY DIFFERENT TYPES OF GUESTS

The first step is to look at the different types of guests that you can expect at your glamping site. You do, however, need to keep in mind whether you have any specific regulations or a very particular target audience for your glamping site. In this case, the general range of guest types may not effectively fit within the standard ones that you can look at. Still, take note of the general guest types that often have an interest in glamping sites to get started here.

- **Business Travelers:** With the rise of glamping, some business individuals who need to travel for work-related purposes consider these sites for accommodation. The great thing about someone traveling for business purposes is the fact that they will often only use the glamping unit to sleep in at night. They will likely be out doing business throughout the day. These visitors generally just want to relax and unwind after a day of meetings and other tasks.

- **Families:** There are also many families who decide to travel to glamping sites. This may include a couple with or without children. Sometimes, the couple may even decide to bring the grandparents along. This is a type of guest that you want to keep an eye on, especially if they are bringing along kids and pets.

- **Senior Citizens:** Some people who retire may decide to travel around in order to experience different sites throughout the world. These seniors are usually quiet and calm. They simply want to experience nature and have a relaxing time.

- **Large Groups:** Sometimes, you may get bookings for large groups. In these cases, consider who the group consists of. When the group consists of many young individuals who might want to throw a party, be careful. This especially accounts for cases where a group of millennials wants to make a booking at your glamping site.

Of course, this list does not cover every type of guest that you may encounter when you manage your own glamping business. Over time, it definitely becomes easier to quickly tell which customers might give you some trouble and be difficult to deal with.

Safety Procedures To Implement

It's generally a good idea to have a series of rules implemented to protect yourself, your staff, and the glamping site you own. This can also help you better understand which clients you might want to refer to a different site when they do not fit the ideal target audience that your glamping site is for.

Still, the risk of having difficult customers come to your glamping site will remain something that you have to keep in mind. This is why you have to ensure you implement a few safety procedures from the very beginning. Stick to these safety procedures and ensure customers comply with them too. This can help to reduce the risk of ending up with a problematic situation due to a guest being difficult.

Below, I am going to discuss a couple of important things that you should use to add more safety procedures to your business and provide better protection for yourself and your glamping site:

- **Rental Agreements:** Even though your guests only stay at your glamping site for a short period of time, it is important to note that this is still a type of rental. This is why you should ensure you implement a rental agreement in order to provide protection against guests that are difficult to deal with. Make sure the rental agreement provides a full overview of the terms and conditions you wish to set out for the people who rent units on your glampsite. These agreements should state the maximum number of people per contract and unit. Provide details about terms related to checking in and out of the glamping site. Make sure you also specify the fact that if the rental agreement is not adhered to, you have the right to cancel the agreement and terminate the reservation that the guest made immediately.

- **Cancellation Policy:** Cancellations can be problematic and even cause you to lose money. This is why you should also add a cancellation policy to the rental agreement. Make sure you send this to the guest as soon as they make the booking. This can help to avoid confusion later on when they do want to make a cancellation on the unit they reserved.
- **Security Deposit:** It is a good idea to ask for a security deposit from all of your guests. In addition to the rental fees for the unit that they want to stay in, charge an extra upfront amount that is required before they can enter your glamping site. This security deposit is refundable. You should keep the security deposit up until the point where you do an inspection when the guests check out. If you find that guests have caused property damage or break anything that is the property of your glamping site, then you should deduct the cost of these problems from the security deposit that the client provided.
- **Rules:** Having fixed house rules for the units you rent out is also something important that you have to attend to. This will depend on what you want and envision for the property. For example, you may specify a time after which no loud noises may be made. This can help to limit the risk of one group making it unpleasant for other guests when they play loud music at night. If you do not want people to smoke at the glamping site, then

mention this on the list of rules you provide them with.

- **Inventory:** When guests decide to keep some of the things that you offer them access to in the units for themselves, you'll need to replace it. While a single replacement may not set you back too much, it can definitely count up over time. This is why taking inventory is important. Make sure you know about every item inside each unit prior to the arrival of guests. Do an inventory check of your glampsite's possessions after guests leave to ensure that everything is still there.

- **Secure Payment Processing:** When you accept payments for a reservation, it is important to use secure payment processing systems. Do not use a payment system that the client can send back or cancel. This causes a higher risk of fraud, where clients stay at your glamping site and then request a refund on the funds they paid after they leave.

- **Guest Reviews:** If you use a platform like Airbnb to scout for guests that want to stay at your glamping site, then take advantage of the reviews provided by other hosts. This is a very useful feature for hosts to determine which guests might prove to be problematic. When you receive a request for a reservation, go to the profile of the guest on the platform you use. Look for any reviews and read through them. Pay close attention to any bad reviews that previous hosts left on the guest's page.

- **Insurance:** I already discussed the topic of insurance in a previous chapter, but want to place some emphasis on this again. Having insurance can provide your property with protection against damage and other issues that you may face. Some insurance products may even pay for property damage caused by a guest. This can help to reduce the expenses you have in these events.

You now have a good idea about the specific maintenance and management procedures you should implement to keep your glamping business running. I discussed the importance of regular maintenance and keeping a cleaning checklist with you in this chapter. You also learned about techniques that can help to provide protection against difficult customers - keeping you and your glamping business safe in the process.

You now have the knowledge you need to set up a glamping business and make it profitable. In the next chapter, you can learn more about a few success stories from others who decided to set up a glamping business too.

Glamping Success Stories

As glamping continues to rise, many people are starting their own glamping businesses. This also means there are many success stories that we can turn to as inspiration - showing us the potential that a glamping business can have, and what we should expect.

In the final chapter of this book, I'm going to discuss a few success stories that really inspired me thus far. You can read about these success stories to help yourself find inspiration and understand how others have also gone from zero to successful glamping business with the right strategies on hand.

Star Field Camping

David and Debby Clark had been operating their country store for decades before the idea of a glamping site came to mind. The country store provided a variety of accessories and animal food that local farmers started to rely on. Over time, Charity Farm, the name of the farm where the country store were operated at, grew and progression was made. At this point, the owners decided to start offering clothes, gifts, and other items that locals found useful.

Following a gathering with their family, the idea of adding a campsite to the farm came up. Since Debby and David already had their hands full, they turned to their daughter for this task. She was able to establish a campsite that offered a traditional camping experience to guests. Debby and David visited a glamping show a while after and felt intrigued by what they saw. This is when the couple decided to add a few glamping facilities to the campsite, now known as Star Field camping. In addition to glamping structures, the property still offers classic camping experiences too - which gives the guests more diversity to choose how they want to spend their time outdoors.

The decision to add these amenities to the property came after the owners noted an increase in local competition, as well as a fall in sales. To make up for the rough time that they faced, a campsite was a perfect idea. They simply required an open field in order to get started - which was already available on Charity Farm.

The owners decided to not make any large alterations to the land when they set up both the campsite and the glamping facilities. This helps to keep things more natural and allows people to enjoy nature as it is, without too many man-made modifications to the layout and structure of the area.

. . .

Something that makes Star Field Camping a great glamping site is its location. The glamping site is located close to a series of different castles, including the popular Sissinghurst Castle. It is also just about an hour's drive from London, which allows guests to easily gain access to the essential services that they may need throughout their stay.

CAMP KATUR

Camp Katur is an excellent example of how expansions to an existing glamping site can help to skyrocket the business and lead to greater success. During the Covid pandemic, many people experienced distress, loss, and difficulty. Depression and similar problems started to rise during these times, which led the owners of Camp Katur to believe that a break from city life and a few days in nature could be the perfect therapy for these individuals.

At the time, Camp Katur already existed as a glamping site. The camp uses stargazing domes for accommodation, which provides a safe environment for guests to sleep. The clear structure at the top of these geodomes allowed guests to watch the stars at night without feeling the cold breeze outside.

The owners decided to make an expansion by adding 12 new FDomes to the property during the pandemic. Two of the domes that the owners decided to add feature en-suite models that help to add a "premium" element to the accommodation guests are able to choose from. These domes allowed Camp Katur to thrive further and offer the perfect escape for people who wanted to take a break and unwind from the stress that a pandemic has placed on the world.

BACKYARD GLAMPING GARDEN

The Backyard Glamping Garden is an inspirational story of how a company was looking to increase its income and ended up with a luxury camping site in its backyard. If you revert back to some of the previous chapters, you'll remember that I already mentioned glamping is versatile enough to be started in your backyard - and then you could even decide to grow from there.

This story relates to the Akwaaba Mansion, situated in New York City. Monique and Glenn Pogue Greenwood decided to buy this 1860 mansion in the year 1995, which they decided to renovate and turn into an inn. The inn offered the guests access to a total of four rooms and primarily focused on serving as a bed and breakfast for many years.

The owners of the inn were looking for ways to increase their profits later on. At the time, the rooms brought in $205 per night each, but due to limitations in the number of rooms, this led to low profitability of the business. The couple who owned the inn decided to approach Chrissy and Erik Kopplin. They are the co-founders of a company called KCC Design + Build, with experience in a variety of construction projects. Following an inspection of the business, Erik and Chrissy noted that the backyard at the mansion was empty and not in use. It had overgrown plants and was not properly attended to - but this also posed as an opportunity.

The two decided to suggest turning the backyard of the inn into a glamping site. They used tents as accommodation, fitted with several luxury elements that would offer guests that perfect glamping experience. Additionally, the couple decided to add a large dining table with several chairs to the backyard. This further increased the amenities that the inn is able to offer guests access to. A few decorative pieces later and the glamping site was ready to start accepting guests.

Collective Retreats

Peter Mack decided to open Collective Retreats after he wanted to combine his love for the outdoors with his expertise in hospitality. He thought the hospitality industry was ready for change and that opening up a glamping site was the perfect opportunity to implement this change.

The initial idea was not a glamping site, however. Peter first considered setting up a hotel to provide accommodation to guests, but the high entry cost for this type of business made it an option that he could not afford. Peter also decided that the costs involved with building a hotel would not help him reach his goal of connecting the people who visit collective retreats to both the environment and the culture of the area.

Collective retreats refer to a collection of different glamping sites that Peter owns today. He started with Collective Vail, which is the very first glamping site that he decided to put up. While tents were used for accommodation, Peter had these tents designed in such a way that they resemble small buildings. This creates a more spacious environment for guests to stay in. Following the opening of the first site, Peter had excellent feedback from his guests who stayed at the glamping site.

This motivated Peter to continue with his efforts and later on expand to have multiple glamping sites that guests can enjoy.

CAMP NUJUM

Camp Nujum is an excellent example of a case where a higher budget can lead to a beautiful site that offers a truly luxurious experience. This type of glamping business is not a great choice for beginners, of course, but it still goes to show just how many opportunities are present within this industry. Camp Nujum is a concept type of glamping business located in Abu Dhabi - more particularly, within the desert. The idea really is something new, but it has taken off quickly and now offers a luxury experience to many guests.

Camp Nujum was developed as a complementary accommodation system for the Qasr Al Sarab Desert Resort. The resort is located in Abu Dhabi and situated close to what is now known as Camp Nujum.

There are several things that make Camp Nujum such an excellent option for people who want to have a glamping experience. The tents offer a wide variety of amenities that contributes to the overall comfort that the guests experience. The guests who stay at Camp Nujum also gain access to camel travel. There are also several activities that people can enjoy, such as archery, sandboarding, and more. There is also a bonfire barbecue that the owner of Camp Nujum organizes for the evenings. This bonfire helps the guests come together and really connect to the environment.

· · ·

While the owner of Camp Nujum wanted to create a luxury experience, he also wanted to avoid having to charge up to $1,000 for a night's stay at the location. With a smart construction plan and proper research, Camp Nujum was able to set up everything that the guests need for a glamping and comfortable experience for a rate that starts at less than $500 per night.

Conclusion

Glamping is considered a multi-million dollar industry and is growing rapidly. As the market is growing quickly, it brings about an opportunity to start a business, but the process of setting up your own site can be a bit daunting. This especially accounts for people with little experience or those who have not worked in any type of tourism, hospitality, or related industry before.

Setting up a glamping business does not have to be such a daunting task. By knowing the right steps to follow throughout the process, things can be easier. In this book, I taught you all the basics that you need to know. Now, the time has come for you to use the information that you gathered in this book and start the process for your own glamping business.

If you found the information and tips that I shared in this book helpful, then I have a quick favor to ask of you. I would sincerely appreciate it if you could take a minute or two to leave a review on the Amazon page of my book. This would really help me reach more people who are passionate about glamping and want to start their own businesses in this industry.

References

- https://www.americaoutdoors.org/rise-of-glamping-market-evolution-trends/
- https://www.inspiredcamping.com/pitahaya-glamping-business-setup-success-manolo-ramos/
- https://www.johnbaileyco.com/glamorous-camping-also-known-as-glamping/
- https://operto.com/glamping-business-profit/
- https://www.glampitect.com/blog/how-much-money-glamping-businesses-make-site-feasibility
- https://glampingspace.com/glamping-accommodation/
- https://glampingnearme.com.au/7-amazing-types-of-glamping-accommodation/
- https://www.starterstory.com/ideas/glamping-business/pros-and-cons
- https://www.canvascamp.com/en_us/how-to-start-glamping-business?utm_source=google&utm_medium=organic
- https://www.glampitect.com/what-weve-done/case-studies/braeview-glamping?hsLang=en
- https://www.tentsxpert.com/blog/what-are-glamping-business-models.html
- https://www.ezeeabsolute.com/blog/starting-glamping-business/
- https://www.igms.com/glamping-business/
- https://www.inspiredcoursesvip.com/blog/buying-a-campsite-or-campground-land-for-glamping
- https://excelitedomes.com/target-market-for-glamping-business/

References

- https://www.uschamber.com/co/start/startup/conducting-competitive-analysis
- https://www.glampitect.com/what-weve-done/case-studies/chid-glamping?hsLang=en
- https://operto.com/glamping-business-plan-template/
- https://www.growthink.com/businessplan/help-center/glamping-business-plan
- https://www.igms.com/vacation-rental-marketing/
- https://howtostartanllc.com/what-is-an-ein
- https://www.enchantedcreations.co.uk/blog/which-glamping-structures-need-planning-permission
- https://howtostartanllc.com/business-insurance/business-insurance-for-glamping-businesses
- https://www.pathwaylending.org/news-and-blog/news/success-story-grandview-mountain-cottages/
- https://glampinghub.com/blog/guide-to-financing-your-glamping-site/
- https://www.starterstory.com/ideas/camping-brand/success-stories
- https://www.enchantedcreations.co.uk/blog/how-to-choose-which-glamping-pods-to-buy-simple-guide-cn66s
- https://www.airstream.com/blog/how-to-shop-for-a-new-airstream/
- https://www.thebusinessbarn.co.uk/rural-business-ideas-and-inspiration/rural-business-case-studies/glamping-site-inspired-by-global-trav
- https://www.lifeintents.com/blogs/the-lit-list/how-to-start-a-glamping-business-creating-a-perfect-glampsite
- https://www.lifeintents.com/blogs/the-lit-list/ideas-for-decorating-a-glamping-tent
- https://www.thebusinessbarn.co.uk/rural-business-ideas-and-inspiration/rural-business-case-studies/glamping-site-inspired-by-global-travel/

REFERENCES

- https://www.rentle.io/blog/ecommerce/how-to-make-a-rental-website
- https://www.greatdwellings.com/post/benefits-of-becoming-an-Airbnb-host
- https://glamping.expert/2019/09/18/greeces-glamping-pioneers-case-study-for-international-glamping-business/
- https://www.bdir.com/news/cleaning-and-maintenance-details-of-glamping-tents
- https://www.guesty.com/blog/how-to-deal-with-bad-guest-reviews/
- https://openairbusiness.com/star-field-camping/
- https://fdomes.com/camp-katur-a-great-example-of-how-to-expand-a-glamping-business-during-a-covid-pandemic%ef%bf%bc
- https://www.cnbc.com/2019/12/31/5-day-biz-fix-turned-overgrown-yard-into-glamping-garden-see-pictures.html
- https://americanglampingassociation.net/news/meet-peter-mack-founder-and-ceo-of-collective-retreats
- https://www.travelweekly.com/Travel-News/Hotel-News/Glamping-next-level
- https://www.glamping.com/what-is-glamping/
- https://www.grandviewresearch.com/industry-analysis/glamping-market
- https://www.businesswire.com/news/home/20220428006026/en/The-Global-Glamping-Market-Will-Grow-to-USD-5.94-Billion-by-2030-at-a-CAGR-of-10.9---ResearchAndMarkets.com
- https://www.americaoutdoors.org/rise-of-glamping-market-evolution-trends/

Printed in Great Britain
by Amazon